# Lighthouses of Chicago Harbor

*Their History, Architecture and Lore*

Chicago Harbor Lighthouse, ca. 1965.
U.S. Coast Guard photo

# Acknowledgements

I'd like to thank the following organizations and institutions whose collections were instrumental in writing this book: The National Archives, Chicago Maritime Society, Chicago Historical Society, Newberry Library in Chicago, Chicago's Harold Washington Library, and United States Coast Guard Archives. These repositories are the guardians of America's documented past and hold the keys to understanding its future.

I'd also like to thank John Stassen, former president of the Landmarks Preservation Council of Illinois, and The Richard Driehaus Foundation for advice and support in producing this publication. In addition, Mr. John Vandereedt at the National Archives and Dr. Robert Browning of the U.S. Coast Guard Archives were of great assistance during a prolonged period of research in Washington DC. I also owe a debt of gratitude to Dr. Theodore Karamanski of Loyola University for his survey, *Historic Lighthouses and Navigational Aids of the Illinois Shore of Lake Michigan.* I'd like to acknowledge help received from Tom Laverty, a friend and manager of New Jersey's Twin Lights Light Station for providing information about Chicago's 1893 Columbian Exposition Lighthouse–a structure that eventually wound up in New Jersey. Tom Griffen of Northeastern Illinois University and Ms. Fanny Guibert of Paris, France, both acted on my behalf in corresponding with the Bibliotheque Nationale de France. David and Mary Dietrich generously shared photos and biographical information on the Davenport family of keepers. Also, veteran Chicago editor, Wayne Siatt, helped with early revisions to this book and Joe Davis was instrumental in assisting with photographs and graphics used herein.

Finally, this book is dedicated to the memory of Jack Terras–a great father. While he may not have shared my interests, he was always supportive of them.

DJT

Chicago Harbor Lighthouse. Photo by D.J. Terras, 2003

# Table of Contents

# Author's Preface

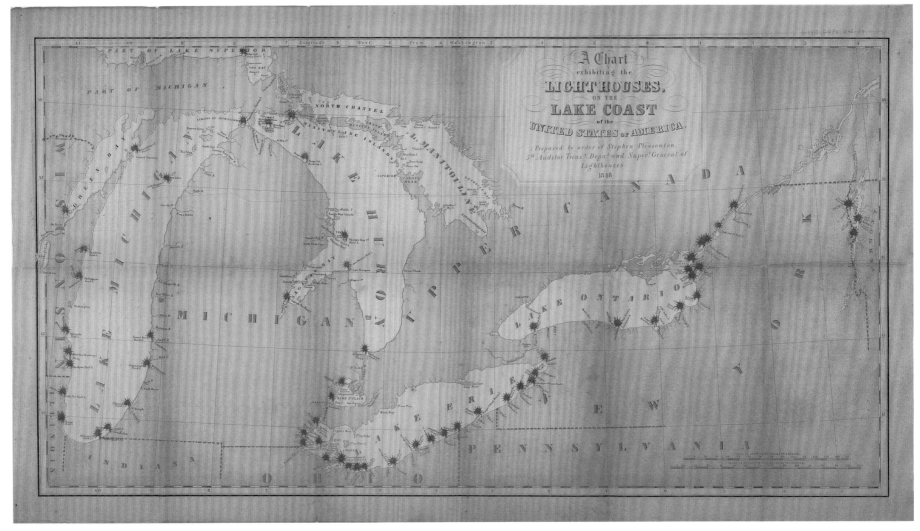

This map of the Great Lakes dates from 1848 and shows the locations of lighthouses built and operated by the federal government through the U.S. Lighthouse Establishment. Like most everything else produced by the Lighthouse Establishment at the time, the name of Stephen Pleasonton figures prominently in the credits. Pleasonton controlled lighthouses through the Department of the Treasury from 1820 until 1852 when, amidst accusations of ineptitude and federal investigations, authority over lighthouses was taken from him and given to a nine–member Lighthouse Board. Under direction of the Board, the number of lighthouses expanded throughout the remainder of the 1800s and into the 1900s as waterborne commerce on the Great Lakes increased and they collectively became a fourth seacoast to the United States. Map courtesy of Eleutherian Mills Historical Society/Hagley Museum.

Lighthouses are a tangible reminder of civilization's entry into uncharted territory. Historically, they stand at the edge between the known and unknown with a beacon of light as guide. In 1832, when the first lighthouse became operational at Chicago Harbor, it was located at the doorstep to the Wild West and the many yet unexplored regions there. Today, most of the world's terrain has been fully charted and through the use of satellite positioning systems, navigators can find their location within several feet anywhere on the globe. This is hardly a technology of romance, but over time the old lighthouses have become romantic in the public eye and this is not likely to change. They appeal to people on a very personal and emotional level and perhaps speak to something that is missing in the lives of the average person today. After studying lighthouses for many years, I find that their attraction to people is somewhat mystical.

More pragmatically, the beacons that guided ships in and out of Chicago's harbors have played a pivotal role in developing the lower Great Lakes region and beyond. The tall lighthouse towers stood as sentinels of safety for those who traversed waterways with shiploads of passengers and cargo destined for all parts of the country. Historically, they represent a period of expansion that encompasses great cultural, scientific and technological advancements in the United States. Indeed, these aids to maritime navigation are part of such advancements and should not be viewed out of context with the commercial and economic success of Chicago and other port cities. In the realm of time and space, knowledge of context adds deeper understanding of history and culture, and it is with this in mind that I've written the following book.

To properly relate the story of lighting Chicago's harbor, it is necessary to explore the history of not only the current lighthouse but others that have preceded it and the circumstances surrounding their construction. It is difficult to appreciate any of this information by presenting one piece of the puzzle and not including others. For a more complete picture one must also delve into the development of maritime Chicago. The early growth of this Midwestern metropolis was linked directly to its geographic location on Lake Michigan and the early pioneers who had a vision that the city would become a pivotal point for receiving and distributing commerce throughout the country.

In fact, Chicago was pivotal to the development of the lucrative lake shipping business during the 1800s and the harbor there was expanded to support an increase in use of port services. Piers were constructed and the Chicago River entrance was widened and made deeper to accommodate larger steamships. Breakwaters were built to protect shipping facilities from Lake Michigan's turbulent waters. Eventually, the Chicago River was connected to an inland waterway network providing access to both the Gulf of Mexico and Atlantic Ocean. Chicago's lighthouses played an important role in this chapter of maritime history in the United States, and the development of Chicago into the 1900s cannot be fully understood without viewing these activities together, acknowledging the city's harbor lights and keepers who faithfully maintained them. The information that is provided in the following pages will give the reader this viewpoint, adding a unique perspective to Chicago's role as the most important historical port on the Great Lakes.

It may seem strange to think that Chicago was at one time a center for maritime activity on a par with the likes of San Francisco or New York City. Those days have departed with the tall schooners and other cargo-carrying sailing ships, but the impact of that period has left an indelible impression on the city. Today, the current Chicago Harbor Light remains on the Coast Guard's list of active aids to maritime navigation and is also listed on the National Register of Historic Places. Automation has taken this station and Chicago's other navigational aids out of the control of light keepers, but their operation continues to be an asset to the many types of vessels that use the harbor. At the same time this lighthouse also serves as a symbol for students of history and culture, representing a present-day connection to the events that shaped the making of Chicago and brought America's maritime heritage to its heartland.

Donald J. Terras

# Introduction

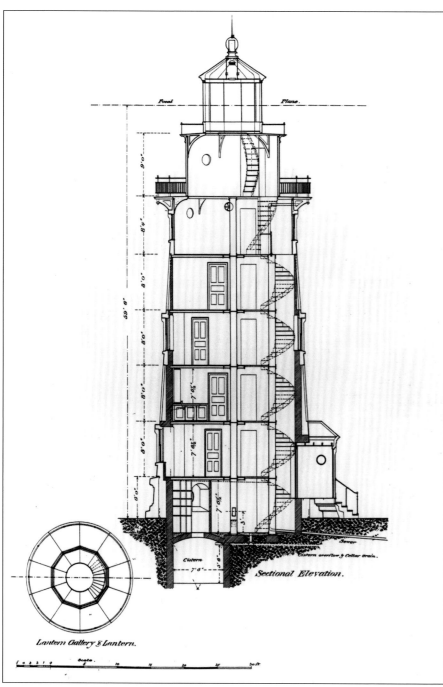

Focal Plane.

Sectional Elevation.

Cistern

Lantern Gallery & Lantern.

Scale

Architectural cross-section of the 1893 Chicago Harbor lighthouse.
Illustration from the National Archives

When we get into our automobiles, drive to the airport, and fly thousands of miles in a matter of hours, we take transportation for granted. It can be difficult to appreciate the fact that throughout the many millennia of human history waterways have been the most efficient method for getting from one place to another. It is only within the last two centuries that tolerable transportation left the water; and it is only in the last seventy-five or so years that moving over the ground and in the air became simple.

Walking, or traveling by horse if you could afford one, was slow, but not necessarily arduous as long as you did not have to carry anything too heavy. Moving goods and commodities overland was another story altogether. Trade was limited by what a horse or wagon could carry, and in the absence of modern roads fording an inconsequential brook could ruin your day or even your entire trip. Settlers moving west over the Great Plains considered fifteen miles of travel a good day. A landscape can look as flat as a billiard table from a distance, but up close it is an endless terrain of ruts, holes, bumps, discomfort, and peril. Mountain ranges were even worse; they were difficult or impossible to go over or around. So effective a barrier to communication are mountains that they played a significant role in the creation of separate languages. Water

provided an easier way to get from one place to another. It was smooth, except for the occasional storm or rapids and, if a vessel were headed downstream, water even provided motive power. Winds on the seas could push a thousand-ton ship more easily than a team of oxen could take a wagon of produce over a mountain. It is for these reasons that all the great cities of the world are located on waterways whether they are the Atlantic or Indian Oceans, the Mediterranean or South China Sea, the Nile, Thames, Hudson, or Mississippi Rivers–or the Great Lakes that connect the Midwest to the rest of the world.

Oceans, lakes, rivers, and even the smallest streams comprised the routes of international and inter-state "highway" systems. Without transportation human society would never have evolved beyond hunting and gathering. The use of these systems required an extensive infrastructure for operations and maintenance. Wharves, piers, warehouses, shipyards, and harbors provided places to receive and send goods and passengers. Locks, dams, canals, weirs, dredges, and breakwaters, kept the water flowing. Marine engineering and astronomy advanced science. Cartography told mariners where they were and how to get to where they were going. Lighthouses were and are a significant part of the vast and ages-old marine transportation network. Lights told sailors where they could find safe water or harbor entrances.

That lighthouses' positive psychological effect imbues them with the symbolic representation of relief should be no surprise. Sextants and global positioning systems are great scientific achievements, but neither is as compelling as a simple beam of light extending over the water. Lighthouses are something special, and their representation of safety and guidance has meaning well beyond the nautical world. On dark nights the first pulsating glow on the horizon tells mariners that the end of the journey is in sight and a safe harbor lies close ahead, welcoming them as if someone left the light on for them. Another literary depiction of lighthouses is, ironically, isolation. A lighthouse keeper is portrayed as a person who lives cut off from the rest of the world except for brief and infrequent contact, an eccentric who lost or is losing the ability to relate to other people. The truth is, however, that most of the workers who tended lighthouses were ordinary people living in metropolitan areas. Many lights serve to mark harbors, which suggests the proximity of a port city. Contrary to the image of lighthouse workers as hermits, most dwelt in or near urban areas and participated in society as trained, responsible technicians.

In use for thousands of years, improvements in navigation and safety diminished the need for lighthouses as the twentieth century progressed.

There are still plenty of lights along the world's waterways to show the way home, but automation has reduced their numbers and all but eliminated the need for traditional keepers. Other advances, such as the substitution of electricity for kerosene, reduced maintenance costs and the number of maintenance workers. Some of the lights were switched off, but the romantic image burned as strong as ever. In response to the potential loss of lighthouses a cadre developed out of those individuals who valued the lights and wanted to see them preserved. Lighthouse preservationists are educators, not antiquarians. Keeping old facilities in good shape gives us a look into outmoded technologies that at one time were among the most advanced that engineering could offer. More than that, however, the research and the programs given to us from those too-few devotees to "lighthouse keeping" is genuine social history focussed sharply on a relatively small group of humans engaged in a critically important activity. The people who perform the tasks necessary to operating the infrastructure systems that produce results we all take for granted are often overlooked. Those overlooked people are both today's lighthouse preservationists and the light keepers of the past.

If one of the purposes of studying history is to show continuity with the past in order to understand the present, then readers ought to be able to understand the relationship between the Grosse Point Lighthouse

of the nineteenth century and the relatively newer lights that mark the Great Lakes today. History can be learned through more than books or documents. History can also be learned through material culture, that is, old buildings and objects. As citizens we should be grateful that a relatively few dedicated professionals have taken up the chore of saving historic material for us so that we can learn more about ourselves. Without knowing anything of the past we are isolated in the present, much as a lonely lighthouse keeper on some faraway, fog-bound promontory. The theme of this book demonstrates the continuities and changes in history that have created the present. The Chicago skyline we see today is the product of yesterday's city. The bright points of light still illuminate our vista.

Theodore W. Hild

Chief of Staff
Preservation Services Division
Illinois Historic Preservation Agency

# Some Notes on the History of Lighthouses

Depiction of the Pharos of Alexandria, Egypt.
Illustration from Thiersch, 1909

The lighthouses that have marked Chicago Harbor are descendants of many others around the country, and the world, that trace their ancestry back thousands of years. In fact, some historians date the existence of lighthouses to the time of the Greek poet Homer (ca. 1200-850 B.C.) and use this stanza taken from his epic, the Iliad, to support their position.

*. . . and then he took the shield,*
*Massive and broad, whose brightness streamed as far*
*As the moon's rays, and as at sea the light*
*Of beacon, placed in some lonely spot,*
*By night, upon a mountain summit shines*
*To mariners, whom the tempest's force has drive*
*Far from their friends across the fishy deep;*
*So from that glorious buckler of the sun*
*Of peleus, nobly wrought, a radiance streamed*
*Into the sky ...*

William C. Bryant's English Translation, 1870

Language and time barriers aside, the Great Poet does seem to be referring to a lighthouse. Other historians are less convinced, however. What we do know is that the generally accepted view of lighthouse history begins late in the 3rd century B.C. when Greeks constructed the great Pharos lighthouse on an island at the entrance to the Port of Alexandria, Egypt. Standing an estimated 400 feet in height, the Pharos welcomed ships into port for some 1500 years before earthquakes brought about its destruction. Other early lighthouses were built by the Romans around the Mediterranean Sea and along the coasts of Spain, France and Britain. Their architecture varied considerably and almost all were used more during the day than at night. Sea travel after dark was treacherous and shipping merchants much preferred the daylight hours where they could spot a plume of smoke from a fire on a light tower more easily than the light emitted by it at night. This changed gradually through the centuries until the design of lighthouse lanterns evolved to the point where the guiding light inside was protected from wind and rain. Eventually, the tops of light towers became enclosed with glass and the light provided for navigation was created through the use of a variety of fuels including whale oil, rapeseed oil, and mineral oil (kerosene).

Great Britain and France led the way in new technologies for lighthouses, and by the 1700s the conical tower we commonly associate with them was being used throughout most of Europe and North America.

The first lighthouse in America was constructed at Boston Harbor in 1716 but was blown up by the British during the Revolutionary War. It was reconstructed in 1783 and continues to operate today, the second oldest lighthouse in the country after Sandy Hook, NJ (1764), a guiding light into New York City.

The spread of lighthouses around North America coincided with an increased flow of immigrants from across the Atlantic Ocean. Soon,

Tour d'Odre or Calligula's Lighthouse, France, 44 A.D. Illustration from Thiersch, 1909.

harbors all along the East Coast of the United States had a lighthouse to aid the growing shipping industry and the westward movement of commerce through inland waterways foretold of the many lighthouses that would be needed to safeguard vessels on the Great Lakes. These lighthouses were at first used only as guides pointing the way into harbors. But as shipping increased, the need to mark treacherous shoals and other natural hazards became apparent and lighthouses soon played an important role as navigational aids for ships in open water.

The illuminating power of lighthouses was greatly enhanced in 1822 with the introduction of the Fresnel lens. Invented by French physicist Augustin Fresnel, the optic installed at the top of the lighthouse was made from glass prisms that magnified the light coming from inside the lens. This created a bright beacon that mariners could spot at great distances over water. It didn't take long for the Lighthouse Board to see the benefits of this new technology and eventually all lighthouses in the United States would come to use the Fresnel system well into the 20th century.

In addition to this change in lighthouse illumination, new construction techniques were developed that enabled engineers to build lighthouses on wave-swept reefs or in mud-bottomed estuaries. The "screwpile" lighthouse is one such design and owes its development to an Englishman by the name of Henry

Eddystone Lighthouse, England, ca.1759 Lithograph from the D.J. Terras Collection

Whiteside who was the first to experiment with so-called pile structures in 1773. Screwpile lighthouses were constructed of stilt-like piles. These piles were screw-shaped at one end and would literally be twisted into a foundation, providing the lighthouse with the stability required to withstand strong winds and turbulent seas. The skeletal design of this lighthouse also presented less of an obstacle to wind and water, which would simply zip through the superstructure. The last half of the 1800s might be called the Golden Age of lighthouse design and construction, for it was during this period that most of America's historic lighthouses were built.

The 1900s ushered in a century of new technological advancements that included the use of electricity in lighthouses and the development of photoelectric cells that would turn the light on and off as needed. By the 1930s, most lighthouses in the United States were electrified and many no longer had light keepers. Lighted buoys offshore became a common and less costly way to mark shipping lanes and shallow water areas, and many lighthouses became surplus property for the federal government. The Chicago Harbor Lighthouse, however, is still maintained as an active aid to maritime navigation—a beacon to the past, illuminating a time in Chicago's history when tall ships roamed the shore and river harbor.

Corduuan Lighthouse, France, 1791.
Illustration from the National Archives

The Boston Lighthouse of 1783 is now part of the Boston Harbor Islands National Park Area.
U.S. Coast Guard photo

# The Great Lakes
Inland Seas of North America

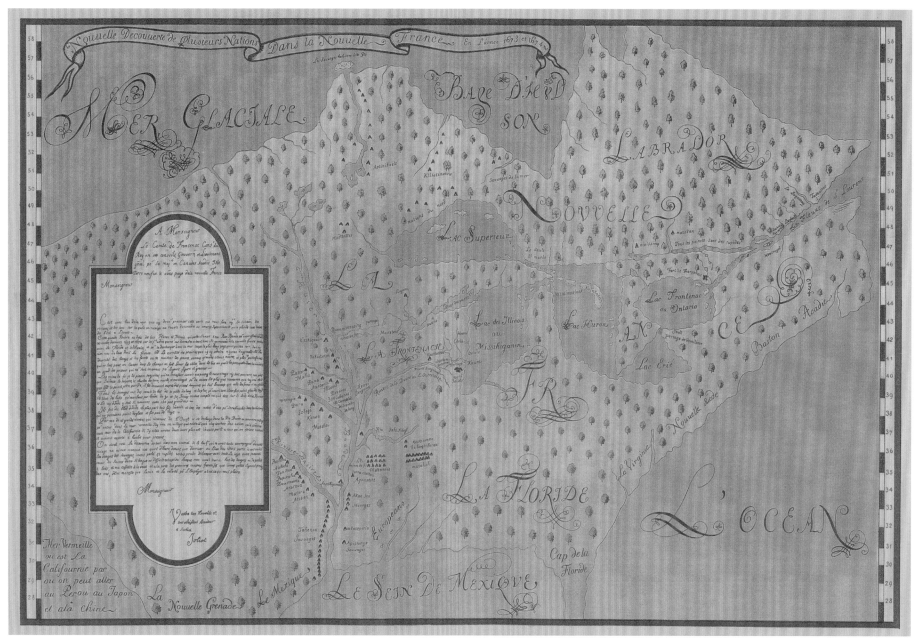

Map of Great Lakes and New France by Louis Joliet, 1674
The noted French explorer and cartographer, Louis Joliet, was the first to foresee an inland waterway transportation network from the East through the Great Lakes to the Mississippi River and south to the Gulf of Mexico. With completion of the Illinois and Michigan Canal in 1848, his vision became a reality.
Map from the National Archives

For those who have never visited the Great Lakes it is difficult to express how expansive they are. Spanning more than 750 miles from west to east, the Great Lakes contain about 5,500 cubic miles of water, covering a total area of about 94,000 square miles. They are the largest system of fresh surface water on earth, containing roughly 18 percent of the world supply. The need to navigate these waters became more pronounced with the development of North America and by 1925 George Weiss, in his book *The Lighthouse Service* (1926), indicates there were 759 lighted aids to navigation of all varieties marking the American shores of the Lakes. According to a survey completed by the National Park Service in 1994 there are over 200 historic lighthouses on the Great Lakes today.

Throughout history the Great Lakes—Superior, Michigan, Huron, Erie and Ontario—have played an important part in the physical and cultural heritage of the entire North American continent. These vast inland freshwater seas have provided drinking water, food, transportation, power, recreation and a host of other uses for Native Americans and European settlers. Populations of Native Americans in the Great Lakes area is estimated to have been between 60,000 and 117,000 in the 17th century, a time when Europeans began their search for a passage to the Orient through the Lakes. Long before white settlement of the region, Native

Americans had been using the Great Lakes and their river tributaries as an inland transportation system. These people accompanied early European explorers, acting as interpreters and guides to the French, British, and Americans who charted the region. Trade between Native Americans and Europeans was important ranging from animal furs, traps, and guns, to more decorative artifacts like glass beads and textiles. In the Chicago area, the Illinois and Pottawattomie cultures were part of a trade network that included other Native American peoples and European settlers throughout the lower Great Lakes.

The first region of the Great Lakes to be visited by Europeans was Georgian Bay in Lake Huron, reached by way of Canada's Ottawa River and Lake Nipissing by the French explorer Samuel de Champlain in 1615 (or possibly Etienne Brule, one of Champlain's scouts, in 1612). The French were able to establish fortresses in the lower St. Lawrence River Valley and regularly used the Ottawa River to penetrate into the heart of the continent. By 1642, the French had established the city of Montreal and went about constructing a series of forts on shores of the western Great Lakes to protect their fur trade. These included Fort Michilimackinac (1670) near the Mission of St. Ignace at the Straits of Mackinac in present-day Michigan; Fort Frontenac (1673), at the site of Kingston, Ontario; and Fort Niagara which was built in 1678

near what is now Youngstown, NY. These important frontier outposts were stopping points for traders who wished to send their products east to Montreal and beyond. The European taste for furs and other items from North America grew considerably throughout the 1700s and Montreal was the chief center of export during this period.

These early years of trade depended to a large degree on the French voyageur canoe, bateau and Mackinaw boat, the latter two representing types of oar-driven watercraft. Free range over all of the Great Lakes was impeded by Niagara Falls (separating Lake Ontario and Lake Erie) and St. Mary's Falls (separating Lake Superior from the lower lakes). Large sailing vessels did not regularly appear until these obstacles were overcome in the 1800s by canals and water locks. The first sailing ship on the Great Lakes, however, was constructed in 1679 west of Niagara Falls near present-day Buffalo, NY, by the famous French explorer Robert Cavelier Sieur de LaSalle. LaSalle named the ship *Griffin* and successfully piloted the craft through Lake Erie, Lake Huron and into Lake Michigan's Green Bay on a trading mission. Unfortunately, this ship was lost on its return journey and has never been found—one of the last great historical maritime mysteries on the Great Lakes.

While the pioneering activity of the French led to their control of much of the fur trade in the Great

Lakes region, British settlement in New England moved westward into the Mohawk Valley in upstate New York and toward the southern shores of the lakes. Eventually, they established Fort Oswego in 1727 on Lake Ontario. Tensions between the British and French were high at this time and reached the breaking point in1756 when the two nations began what has become known as The Seven Years' War in Europe and the French and Indian War in America. Their first American naval engagement was fought on the Great Lakes with the French winning the opening round but eventually losing the war in 1763. Afterwards, the British maintained control of the Great Lakes during the American Revolutionary War, but the lakes themselves became an important part of the boundary between the new United States and what remained of British North America. When the British and Americans finally ceased hostilities after the War of 1812, they agreed on a boundary through the Great Lakes between Canada and the United States that we observe today.

Throughout the 1800s, development of the Great Lakes region continued and was aided by construction of the Erie Canal in 1825. This 364-mile waterway created a link between the Atlantic Coast and Lake Erie, carrying settlers west and freight east. Completion of the canal resulted in a more efficient transportation system, lowering the cost of goods in the west by 90 percent and opening East Coast markets to Midwestern

Early trade on the Great Lakes depended to a large extent on over-sized canoes used by the French voyageurs in their fur trading expeditions. This painting of such a "canot du maitre" by Mrs. F.A. Hopkins illustrates their carrying capacity. From the National Archives of Canada C 27716

agricultural products. The westward terminus of the canal was at Buffalo, NY, and it was here that one of the earliest lighthouses on the Great Lakes was constructed. In 1848 the Illinois-Michigan Canal was completed and waterborne commerce was expanded west to the Mississippi River and south to the Gulf of Mexico.

The best means of transport over the Great Lakes during this time was by sailing craft, and there were several different types registered by the mid-1800s. An increase in the number of these ships helped spur economic development of the area even though their cargo-carrying capacity was

generally limited to 100 tons. Still, the expanded trade network made settlement in the fertile expanses of the Midwest even more attractive, and travel routes through the Great Lakes soon became major highways for moving goods and people. The land that had provided wealth in the form of furs and agricultural products also yielded lumber, and logging operations became a major part of the economy in Michigan, Minnesota and Wisconsin. Sailing vessels played a pivotal role in moving this raw material on the Great Lakes to destinations like Chicago, Milwaukee, Detroit and Cleveland. In addition, ships powered by steam became commonly used for transporting mail and passengers. As a result, the waterborne routes that were used and their cities of destination became well marked with lighthouses. During the 1870s, however, the nation's railway system evolved into a more economically efficient way to move people and commerce. Sail powered vessels would continue to transport lumber into rapidly growing cities like Chicago, but their days were numbered with expansion of train routes and development of the trucking industry in the early 1900s. Commerce would eventually be moved across the country much more effectively by a rapidly growing system of roadways. In addition, there was an increase in the number and size of iron-hulled vessels on the lakes that specialized in moving cargoes of iron ore, limestone and coal. At first the capacity of these vessels to carry cargo was relatively small, but by the early to middle 1900s these ships had grown in size until their cargo compartments would accommodate thousands of tons of commerce. With the opening of the St. Lawrence Seaway in 1959, a direct link was created between waters of the North Atlantic and the Great Lakes. Port cities like Chicago began service for ships from every maritime nation and beacons from their lighthouses served as ambassadors, safely welcoming mariners from around the world into harbors on the Great Lakes–America's fourth seacoast.

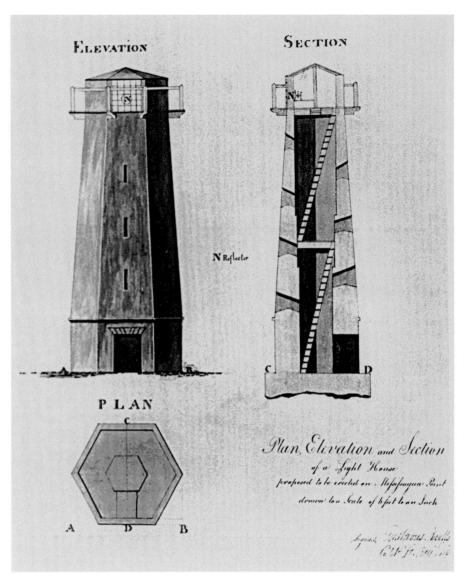

Lighthouse on the Niagara River, 1804.
Illustration from the National Archives of Canada C 27667

The Niagara River, which joins Lake Ontario to Lake Erie and the western Great Lakes, served as an important harbor and base of shipping operations during the early British Colonial period and for many years after. However, the 162-foot drop of nearby Niagara Falls constituted a major obstacle for ships to overcome in traversing the lower Great Lakes. Initially, a portage was used from nearby Fort Niagara to move people and commerce around the waterfalls. But, eventually, the Erie and Welland canals provided routes to circumvent this obstacle.

In fact, the first light to aid maritime navigation on the Lakes was erected on the roof of Fort Niagara in the early 1780's. Very little is known of this structure, but it was replaced by the British in 1804 with a substantial octagon–shaped stone light tower some 45 feet in height that was located at Mississauga Point. This light lasted for 10 years and was replaced with lighthouses constructed by the United States.

# The Port of Chicago: History and Development

In 1869 Chicago's river harbor was filled with tall sailing ships on a daily basis, their hulls bursting with supplies for a growing metropolitan city. Although steamships brought Chicago's settlers, schooners were the main transport for food, manufactured goods and building material. In 1868, more than a billion and a half board feet of lumber arrived in port according to the Annual Report of the Public Works Department. The schooners were far less expensive to operate and needed no fuel or special engineering staff found on steamships.

The sailing ships that came to Chicago were generally blocky in shape for large carrying capacity, rather than sharp-lined for speed. And there were many different varieties including brigs, barkentines, brigantines, barques, topsail schooners and others. This age of sail lasted into the early 1900s but eventually became outdated as newer modes of transportation continued to develop. Photo courtesy of the Chicago Historical Society

It is difficult to imagine a time when the banks of the Chicago River were lined by scores of tall-masted schooners and steamships. Yet, for the last half of the 1800s and early years of the 1900s, this body of water was home to one of the most commercially important ports in the United States, and one of America's greatest cities was to grow there. It wasn't until the 1600s, however, that the history of this area began to be documented by French voyageurs that traversed the inland waters of North America.

In 1673, French cartographer Louis Joliet and missionary Jacques Marquette became the first Europeans to chart the Mississippi River. They traveled south as far as the Arkansas River then returned north over the Illinois River using tributaries that led to a swampy, mosquito-infested backwash of land. Carrying their canoes a short distance, the group took to a small river and were soon gazing at the open waters of Lake Michigan. Joliet made special note of this location because of its strategic importance for military activities, while European fur trappers who followed in his footsteps were more interested in exploiting the area's natural resources. However, because of the difficulties in travel and hostilities with Native Americans, it was not until 1803 that the federal government decided to establish a presence in the area by building Fort Dearborn. This military outpost anchored trade activities in the lower Great Lakes during the early years of

Euro-American expansion across the Midwest and led to increased settlement in the Chicago area.

Many people, however, were not so impressed with the potential of this frontier outpost. A.T. Andreas in his *History of Chicago* (1894) mentions that government mineralogist William Keating made the following comment in 1823.

*The communication will be limited, the dangers of navigation on the lake, the scarcity of harbors, must ever prove a serious obstacle to the increase of the commercial importance of Chicago. Indeed, when the game is gone, it is doubtful that even the Indians will reside here much longer.*

A change in attitude came in 1825 when the Erie Canal was completed, providing access to East Coast ports from the Great Lakes. Soon, a steady flow of passengers and commerce was crisscrossing these inland seas. The outpost at Fort Dearborn in Chicago was the end of the line for a majority of people, many of whom chose to live in the area to take advantage of business opportunities. These pioneers recognized that the fledgling community had the potential to become an economic powerhouse because its location was at a pivotal point for distributing commerce throughout the United States. However, sandbars were an almost constant problem in the early years of Chicago's port activities and blocked the entrance to the river. As early as 1818, soldiers from Fort Dearborn were ordered to dig a ditch through

the sand bar to the lake and release some of the river water to create a new channel. This was only a temporary quick fix and soldiers stationed at the fort found themselves with "ditch duty" for many years until Congress finally began appropriating money for more practical solutions to the problem. To the soldiers' credit, their ditch digging was the beginning of Chicago Harbor.

Eventually, the Chicago River shoreline was developed and served as the location for port facilities as well

entrance was once again blocked by sand, however, and the vessel had to be dragged over dry land before being able to re-enter the water. This sand bar was eventually removed later in the year and the schooner *Napoleon* was able to navigate out of harbor for a trading voyage east. Gradually, settlers moved to the area in increasing numbers and on March 4, 1837, with a population of some 4,170 inhabitants, Chicago was incorporated as a city.

Chicago's port operations during these early years continued to be

Map from Andreas, 1894.

as a much-needed harbor of refuge for ships and passengers. In 1831, three ships arrived at Chicago only to find that a sand bar blocked the port entrance forcing the passengers with their supplies to use a small boat to reach shore. In 1833, the yacht *Westward Ho* became the first vessel larger than a rowboat or a canoe to enter Chicago's river harbor. The

plagued by sandbars that would limit access to the river shoreline and dockside harbor facilities. Vessels were forced to continue the practice of anchoring offshore and moving their cargoes and passengers to the mainland in small boats.

Fortunately, the federal government recognized the potential of Chicago's harbor and appropriated

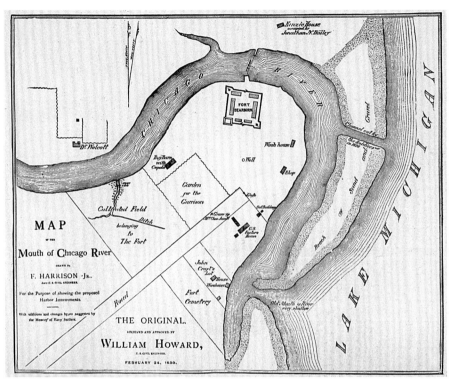

This illustration of the Chicago River, ca. 1830, clearly shows why early navigators had such trouble in gaining access to the waterway. In particular, a pesky sand bar was an almost constant problem. As a result, soldiers posted at nearby Fort Dearborn dug a channel through the sand in an effort to give vessels more direct access to the river and, in 1832, a lighthouse would be built near the fort. Unfortunately, sand continually filled the channel and the lighthouse proved almost useless as it was located too far inland from the river entrance for mariners to spot. Eventually, piers were constructed through the sand bar and a number of lighthouses would come to mark the entrance to Chicago's harbor. Map from the National Archives

money for construction of two piers that were built through the sandbars, creating a channel some seven feet deep and 200 feet wide. However, it was only a matter of time before wind, wave and current created a third sand bar beyond the piers. By 1844, this sand bar problem had become a spending problem. With total appropriations for maintenance of Chicago Harbor at $247,000 Congress began to tire of paying for engineering solutions that were not effective.

Despite different pier designs sandbars continued to hamper navigation into a port that had to be constantly dredged to alleviate the blockage. In 1847, the north channel pier was extended to a length of 3,900 feet and was finally far enough out in the lake to prevent sandbars from blocking the river entrance. In addition, improvements were made to deepen the shipping channel for use by larger lake transports. This solution would seem to have come just in time, for pioneer movement across the country was made easier in 1848 with completion of the Illinois and Michigan Canal, forming a link between Lake Michigan and the Illinois and Mississippi Rivers. Chicago's harbor was soon brimming with activity as businesses flourished and the city's population increased. The river and lake suffered, however, as pollution became a problem. The city's water supply eventually became contaminated, killing thousands of

people in cholera and typhoid epidemics. In an age when pollution control was not a prime issue, Chicago simply handled the situation by lengthening its freshwater intake pipe so that it stretched for two miles from shore into Lake Michigan. In addition, and perhaps more importantly, the Illinois and Michigan Canal was deepened and by 1871 water began to flow southward out of Lake Michigan instead of into the lake. This had a tremendous effect on improving water quality for the city. As one resident responded: *"Then there was the river–the horrible, black, stinking river of a few weeks ago, which has since become clear enough for fish to live in, by reason of the deepening of the canal, which draws to the Mississippi a perpetual flow of pure water from Lake Michigan."*

Because of better living conditions in the city and transportation to and from the productive farmland around it, Chicago's port facilities became the most extensive and productive on the Great Lakes. Its hinterland eventually became the most productive area of large-scale commercial agriculture in the world, producing a surplus for export. Chicago itself was an important market for manufactured goods directly imported from other parts of the country and overseas. The end result was a tremendous boom in the shipping industry that relied on Chicago's harbor and shipping lanes to transport commerce. Soon, the western

Sydney S. Durfee, Chicago's 1st Harbor Master had maps or charts made for mariners. The following description comes from a chart of Chicago Harbor contained in the National Archives.

*Vessels entering the harbor with a northerly wind, should keep the end of north pier close abroa`d, heading southwest or west southwest until they pass the end of the pier, allowing lee way of current and sea setting out past it. They should then haul up for the north pier. The buoy southeast of the extremity of the pier, is at the north end of a sand bar or hill, in nine feet of water. This bar is 200 feet in length and 100 feet in width, rising abruptly in about 16 feet of water.*

*The buoy southwest of the end of the pier is at the northeastern extremity of a middle ground in 8 1/2 feet of water. Steamboats may fall below the first buoy, and head for the light on the pier, when it bears northwest by north where they will find a channel and deep water. Having passed the second buoy, they will head south of the center of the opening of the piers. Vessels drawing nine and three-fourths or ten feet of water can come to south pier, and nine feet within it.*

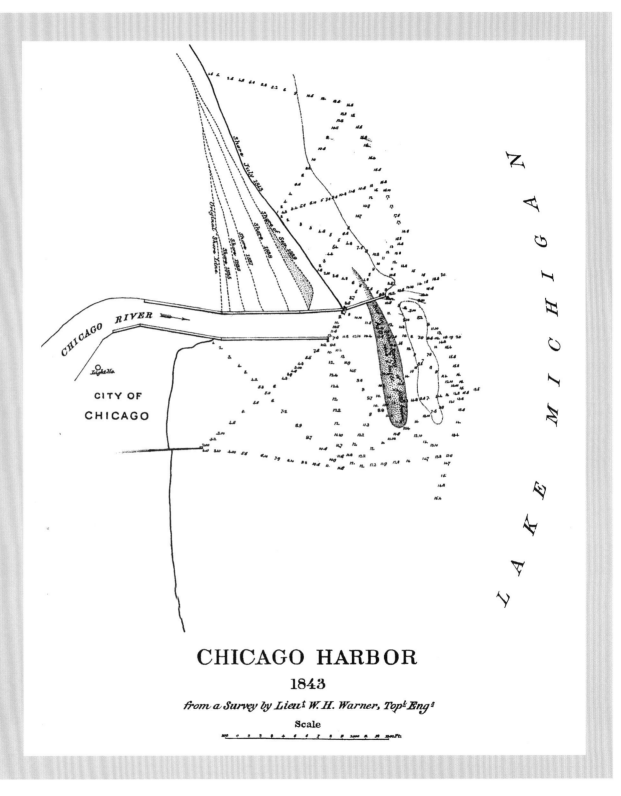

# CHICAGO HARBOR
## 1843
*from a Survey by Lieut. W. H. Warner, Topl. Engs.*

### Scale

states and territories were transformed into the grain basket of the industrial Northeast and Great Lakes sailing ships were a key link in the food chain.

During this time the Port of Chicago, with its weather-shortened eight-month shipping season, soon rivaled and surpassed the year-round ports of New York City, Boston, and San Francisco, as the busiest center for maritime commerce in the country.

This growth continued into the 1880s and it wasn't long before heavy industry began to develop in the city, with large steamships replacing schooners as the major water transport on the lakes. By the 1890s, the Port of

Chicago spread for 18 miles along the north and south branches of the Chicago River. Pollution again became a problem but was effectively handled with the opening of the Chicago Sanitary and Ship Canal in 1900. This skillfully constructed tributary enabled engineers to completely reverse the flow of the Chicago River out of Lake Michigan, a feat recognized by many historians as one of the technological

wonders of the Industrial Age. The polluted water was then treated at purification plants along this inland waterway. When the Sanitary and Ship Canal project was completed, it constituted the main water link between the Great Lakes and Mississippi River and required more land excavation than constructing the Panama Canal.

This period saw Chicago's harbor play a significant role in the maritime commerce of the United States as it became the center of trade for lumber and grain merchants, textile industries, newspaper plants, meat processing facilities and many other businesses that served America. Ironically, at the same time, the city of Chicago was growing away from its maritime past as it became the hub of the railroad and other industries. The city's population swelled and the busy streets would be held up for long periods of time as bridges were raised to accommodate large ships. Army engineers finally agreed that the Chicago River was taxed to its limit and the federal government created a second port facility at Calumet, a relatively undeveloped harbor 11 miles south of the city. The creation of the Calumet and Chicago Canal and Dock Company in 1869 is an indication of the close working relationship between the two harbors serving Chicago. And the construction of the Calumet-Sag Canal created a western link with the Illinois and Michigan Canal and a northern connection to the Chicago River.

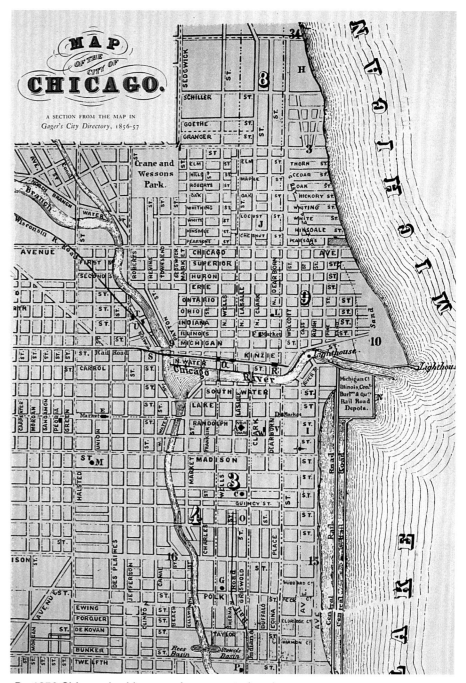

By 1856 Chicago had become incorporated and development expanded her borders far from the river harbor. Map from the National Archives

CHICAGO RIVER, RUSH STREET BRIDGE.

This post card image of a crowded Chicago River dates from 1910. By the early 1900s, there was very little sail traffic in Chicago's harbor, which had been all but taken over by various types of steamships.
From the collection of D.J. Terras

The steel industry moved operations to Calumet in the 1880s and the bulk of Chicago's commerce soon followed. By 1916, commerce in and out of Calumet Harbor surpassed Chicago's river port trade by a five to one ratio. Calumet eventually became one of the greatest centers of heavy industry in the world and Chicago formally adopted the harbor as an additional port.

The movement of industry from Chicago's river port to Calumet had a decided impact on the Chicago shore of Lake Michigan. By the late 1800s most lakefront land in cities bordering the Great Lakes had been snapped up by industry. But in Chicago there was a prevailing philosophy that the lakefront should remain free from business and industry. Architect and city planner Daniel Burnham spearheaded this idea that culminated in 1909 with Burnham's *Plan of Chicago*. In his plan, Burnham stated that *"The lake-front by right belongs to the people. It affords their one great unobstructed view, stretching away to the horizon, where water and clouds seem to meet... Not a foot of its shores should be appropriated by individuals to the exclusion of the people."* Eventually Burnham's plan was adopted by the city and Chicago's accessible lakefront has become a hallmark feature of the metropolis.

Today, Chicago's port facilities are multifaceted with many types of installations to serve vessels on the Chicago River, Illinois Waterway, Lake Michigan and Calumet River. In fact, Chicago serves three major types of commercial traffic: ocean-going vessels through the St. Lawrence Seaway, land-locked bulk carriers on the Great Lakes and barges on the inland water-way system. From the standpoint of access to commerce, it is widely conceded that the advantage of Chicago's geographic location is one shared by no other city in the world.

In addition, there are many small city lakefront harbors filled with pleasure boats of every kind giving Chicago one of the great urban recreational waterfront areas in the world.

Chicago Harbor and vicinity, 1899. Map from the National Archives

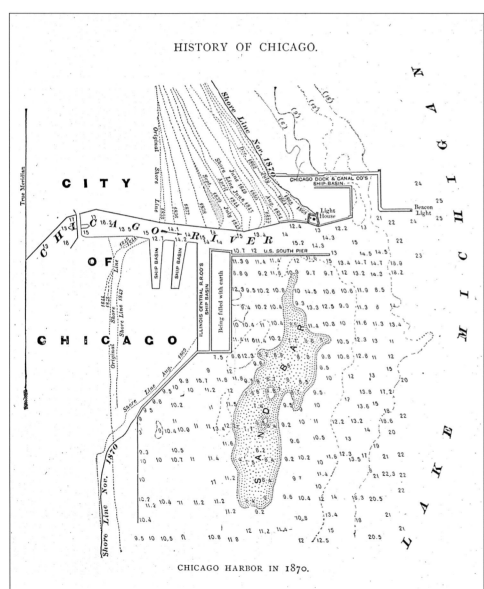

View of Chicago Harbor, 1870. From A.T. Andreas, 1894

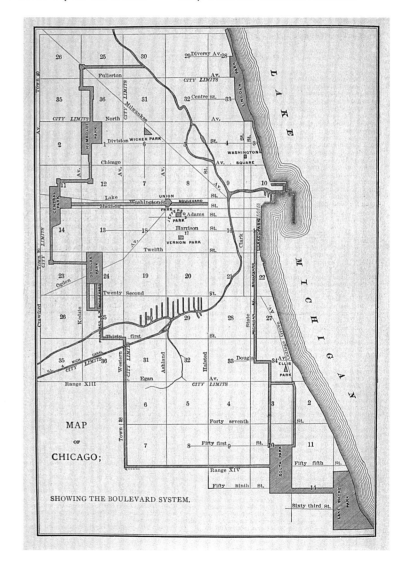

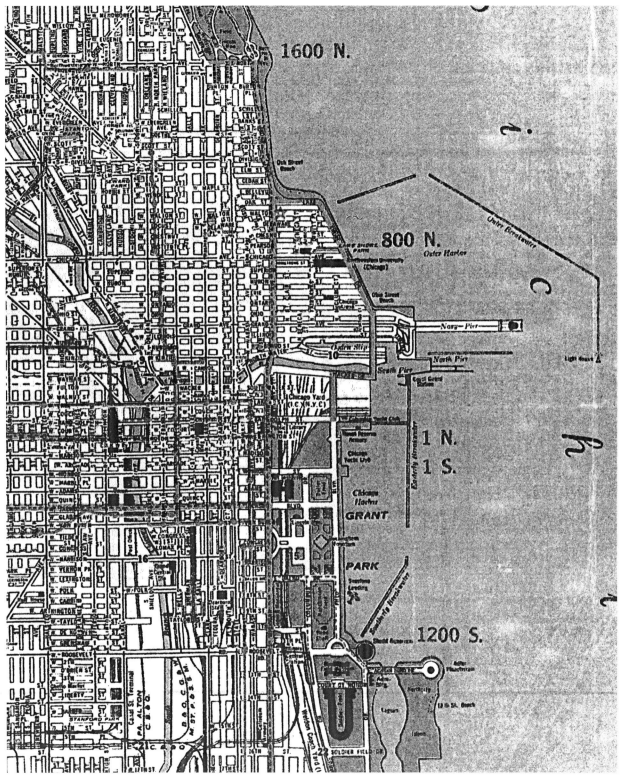

Chicago Harbor and surroundings in 1920. Construction of Navy Pier in 1916 at the mouth of the Chicago River made it the dominant feature along Chicago's lakefront.
Map from the National Archives

# Historic Inland Ports of the U.S.

Daniel Burnham's Plan of Chicago was a bold initiative that has left several notable landmarks in the Windy City. At the lakefront, Burnham envisioned a series of parks with recreational harbors on the mainland and two great piers to enclose the central port area. Outer Harbor Municipal Pier No. 2 was completed in 1916 and is today known as Navy Pier. In its early years, the pier was a favorite place for public events. During World War II, it became a naval training station. For nearly 20 years after the war, it housed the Chicago branch of the University of Illinois. Today, it serves as a major exposition center and place for public entertainment.

MUNICIPAL PIER

Photo of Navy Pier ca. 1930. From the U.S. Coast Guard

## BUFFALO, NY

Like Chicago, the original settlement of Buffalo began in 1804 as a trading post. The small village consisted of a handful of cabins and people at the junction of Lake Erie and the Niagara River. At the time there was no harbor on Lake Erie, which forms a shallow unprotected bay at Buffalo. Early port activities took place along the banks of the nearby Buffalo River, that flows into Lake Erie. The federal government took note of the importance of establishing a port here and on March 3, 1805, designated Buffalo a U.S. Port of Entry providing much-needed official recognition to help aid development.

Expansion of harbor facilities and businesses were given a boost in 1819 when Buffalo was under consideration by the federal government as the terminus of the projected Erie Canal. In an effort to make their harbor more desirable, the people of Buffalo hurried to improve the facility in order to influence the decision of the canal builders. These improvements were partially funded with a state loan in the amount of $12,000. The amount of money was hardly enough and Buffalo–at the time with fewer than 20,000 inhabitants–tried a public subscription drive obtaining some $1,361 in pledges for harbor work, although only $110 of the pledges actually materialized. Further complications arose when the chief harbor engineer was fired for incompetence. Finally, a local judge took over the construction project and the enterprise proved successful. The necessary improvements were made and the mouth of the Buffalo River was chosen as the outlet of the Erie Canal. By 1825, the canal was completed and the port experienced rapid growth.

Much of Buffalo's prominence in industry and trade is attributable to its geographic location, which early in the life of the United States made the city an important stop on the route West. With completion of the canal, Buffalo became an important transshipment point for East-West traffic. Over time, the basis of its existence gradually switched from the canal to the Great Lakes and by the end of the 1800s, Buffalo was the world's seventh busiest harbor.

The port's first main activity was the storage and transport of grain but by the early 1900s, iron and steel manufacturing were introduced with the greatest volume of traffic consisting of bulk commodities such as iron ore concentrates, limestone, coal, petroleum products and lumber. Interestingly, measured in nautical miles, the Port of Buffalo through the St. Lawrence River and Seaway is closer than New York City to such international ports as Belfast, Stockholm, Helsinki, Copenhagen and Hamburg.

Today, Buffalo's local industries still use large amounts of lake-shipped grain, cement, ore and foundry sand. However, commercial port activity is in decline and like Chicago in the early 1900s, the waterfront is increasingly being used and developed for recreational activities.

BUFFALO, FROM LAKE ERIE.

Buffalo Harbor ca. 1835 as painted by W.J. Bennett.
Illustration from the I.N. Phelps Stokes Collection of the New York Public Library

## DETROIT, MI

Detroit is perhaps the city best situated for taking advantage of commerce that flowed through the Great Lakes during the 1800s. Its location on the 29-mile stretch of the Detroit River, between Lake Huron to the north and Lake Erie to the south, made this area important for water-borne traffic traveling the lower and upper Great Lakes. Louis Joliet first charted the land here in 1669, and the French soon realized the strategic advantage of controlling the Detroit River both from an economic and military standpoint. Antoine de la Mothe Cadillac, commandant of the important post of Michilimackinac located in the straits between Lake Michigan and Lake Huron, went to France in 1699 and obtained authorization to establish a fortified settlement at the *"Place du detroit,"* meaning the place of the strait. On July 24, 1701 he and more than 100 soldiers and explorers reached the wooded shores where Detroit now stands. The fortified community there was first called Fort Pontchartrain, in honor of the French Minister of Marine at the time. The name, how-ever, did not last long as people continued to refer to the community as Detroit. Throughout the 1700s, Detroit's importance as a place of trade increased under French control. In 1760, at the end of the French and Indian War, Detroit was captured by British forces that commanded this strategic outpost until 1796 when it was evacuated. Under American control, Detroit was incorporated as a town in 1802.

With the growth of commerce in and around Lake Michigan from the 1830s on and the opening of the Soo Locks in 1855 providing greater access to the lower lakes from Lake Superior, Detroit flourished and served as a convenient supply point for provisions throughout the 1800s. Rapid industrialization came by way of the auto industry and took the port city through the 1900s. Today, the 35-acre port complex runs 2,150 feet along the Detroit River with facilities that can accomodate up to three vessels as large as 1000 feet in length. Manufactured goods are shipped to Europe and the United Kingdom. However, more than 80 percent of the port's total tonnage consists of bulk commodities such as coal, iron ore and cement. In addi-tion, the port is also a place of transshipment for auto parts, lumber and agricultural items.

## DULUTH, MN

The combined cities of Duluth, Minnesota, and Superior, Wisconsin, share the same harbor on Lake Superior and are often referred to as the "Twin Ports." Located nearly 2,300 freshwater miles from the Atlantic Ocean, this harbor is the farthest port west on the Great Lakes.

Duluth became important as an inland port primarily because of its proximity to Minnesota's Vermilion, Cuyuna and Mesabi iron ranges, the sources for most of the iron ore produced in the United States. Long before this time, however, French fur traders were active in the area and in 1669 Daniel Gresolon, Sieur Duluth, the French explorer that the city takes its name from, visited the region. Duluth was not chartered as a town until 1857 and was finally incorporated as a city in 1870. Duluth has an excellent natural harbor about 19 square miles in area and almost completely landlocked. Broad channels enclosing the harbor afford entrance to it and large vessels drawing up to 22 feet of water have access to all parts of the port.

Travel to the lower Great Lakes was, however, restricted by rapids and a waterfall of 19 feet on the St. Mary's River. This effectively cut off open navigation between Lake Superior and

Great Lakes cargo transport vessel passing Detroit's river lighthouse into harbor, ca. 1994.
Photo courtesy of Kurt Spitzer

Split Rock Lighthouse is arguably one of the most picturesque on the Great Lakes. Constructed in 1909, it acted to help vessels navigate waters around Two Harbors Minnesota, just north of Duluth Harbor.
Photo Courtesy of the Minnesota Historical Society

the lower Great Lakes for many years. The only way movement of cargo could be accomplished was for ships to unload their goods on the shorelines where laborers would have to push, shove, roll or drag the supplies for a mile before they could again be picked up by ship and moved along.

The construction of a nine-foot lock in 1797 permitted small vessels to get around the waterfalls, but this was hardly large enough to accommodate the ships needed to develop commercial interests in the area. This situation changed with the opening of the St. Mary's Falls ship canal in 1855 and the construction of large locks at Sault St. Marie, the terminus of the canal.

This passage around the rapids and falls permitted ship traffic on Lake Superior to access ports on all of the Great Lakes, and commerce was soon booming in the area during the latter part of the 1800s. This was due in large part to the steel industry. In 1892, the Port of Duluth shipped 2000 tons of hematite, a mineral important in the manufacture of steel, from the Port of Duluth. By 1910, 25 million tons were shipped. In an eight-month shipping season the Sault Ste. Marie canals at the outlet of Lake Superior handled four times the cargo carried by Egypt's Suez Canal, connecting the Mediterranean Sea with the Red Sea south to the Indian

Ocean. Much of the iron ore carried by these ships was destined for Chicago's Calumet port and the nearby processing facilities of the U.S. Steel Company. Today, Duluth's port remains one of the most important on the Great Lakes and continues to act as a major center for export of iron ore and a variety of other products.

The *D.O. Mills* enters the ship canal in Duluth's harbor, ca. 1908.
Photo from the National Archives

# Great Lakes Navigation and Shipwrecks at Chicago Harbor

The *David Dows* shown here in the Weitzel Lock at Sault Saint Marie, MI, ca.1881.
Photo courtesy of the Chicago Maritime Society

Even with lighthouses and other navigational aids to guide mariners, travel on the Great Lakes was–and still is–hazardous. When Herman Melville took up his pen to write *Moby Dick*, he paid homage to these inland seas through the eyes of his character, Ishmael.

> Now, gentlemen, in their over-flowing aggregate, these grand fresh-water seas of ours–Erie, and Ontario, and Huron, and Superior, and Michigan–possess an ocean-like expansiveness. They contain round archipelagoes of romantic isles. They are swept by Borean and dismasting waves as direful as any that lash the salted wave. They know what shipwrecks are; for, out of sight of land, however, inland, they have drowned many a midnight ship with all its shrieking crew.

Even today, the sophisticated technology carried on vessels is not complete insurance against disaster and large ships are lost from time to time. Lake Michigan has a reputation as being one of the most dangerous of the five Great Lakes. A bright sunny day can become cloudy and turn stormy in very little time. And when a strong northwesterly wind blows down the length of this relatively shallow lake, great waves are quickly created that cause tremendous water turbulence.

Navigating a ship powered by sail or steam through these inland seas during the 1800s was even more demanding. Despite what were considered to be adequate safety precautions at the time, waterborne travel to southern Lake Michigan was a risky venture. In J.B. Mansfield's *History of the Great Lakes* (1899), Englishman Charles J. Latrobe, visiting these waters for the first time early in the 1800s, made the following observation: *"The total absence of harbors round this southern extremity of the Lake has caused the wreck of many a vessel...as the action of the storm from the northward upon such a wide expanse of fresh water is tremendous; and from the great height and violence of the surf, which then thunders in upon the base of the sand hills, and the utter solitude of this coast, lives are seldom, if ever, saved."*

Unlike travel on the oceans, the landlocked waters of the Great Lakes presented special problems for the captain of a sailing vessel to overcome. In stormy weather land is very often too close and blustery winds blowing from the south or northeast sent many ships against a rocky shore or into shallow water where they would be stranded. In these conditions shipmasters had to be well aware of their position relative to land and be prepared to set all sails, drop the centerboard, and plot a course away from shore. A sailing ship foundering under the weight of a storm trying to enter harbor might find itself in conditions that could 'jerk the sticks right out of her' and steam-powered vessels with their coal and wood burning furnaces might fall victim to fire. Legends have it that some of these great storms arose blowing vessels out of one lake, through the air, and into another lake. There were also tales of mysterious disappearances where ships sailed out of port under normal conditions and were never seen again, leaving no trace of the fate that overcame them. Stories of ghost ships were also common and grew out of the sighting of mirages. Under the right conditions, a vessel sighted on a distant horizon might seemingly sail through the air above water. At times sand dunes, forested headlands and other shore features have been seen drifting above water.

Over the years, shipping disasters of all kinds have taken place off the doorstep of Chicago Harbor and the history of lower Lake Michigan holds accounts of vessels that perished in many different ways. The stories of the *David Dows*, *Eastland*, *Flora M. Hill* and *Favorite* are but a few examples of the many tragedies that occurred in these waters.

**Sinking of the *David Dows***

One of the most beautiful ships to ever sail on the Great Lakes was the topsail schooner, *David Dows*. Built in Toledo, Ohio, in 1881, the Dows was the largest schooner in the world at the time it was launched and was an experiment to see if an ocean-sized ship might be profitable on the Great Lakes. It was 278 feet long and 38 feet across the broadest part of her deck. The largest of her five masts was 140 feet above water and the ship carried 19 working sails that needed 70,000 yards of canvas. The ship was massive and fast, and was designed to be a cargo vessel for grain and coal on the Great Lakes, helping an upstart port at Toledo compete with markets dominated by the Port of Chicago.

The *Dows* was designed with two centerboards to make her easier to handle. Unfortunately, when the time came to install those centerboards, the builders discovered that there was not enough water at the Ohio shipyard to float the vessel and it had to be moved to another location in order to be completed. This was perhaps an omen that the ship's builders should have noted, for most harbors on the Great Lakes were not deep enough to accommodate a vessel of her size that was filled to capacity. In short, the ship was designed most of all to make money and the owner's expectations were set too high. For all of her large carrying capacity and quickness the *Dows* proved unwieldy, cumbersome and dangerous. In 1883, only two years after her launching, the *Dows* was reduced to a tow barge. In what was a sign of things to come, the ship-builder of the *Dows* went bankrupt the year following her construction and the eight-year record of the ship on the Great Lakes is filled with mishaps that include a nautical drag race on Lake Erie just months after her launching. This unfortunate incident involved the schooners *C.K. Nims* and *John B. Merrill*, as well as the *Dows*. All three ships were headed from Toledo to Buffalo and decided to make a race of it to add a bit of excitement to an otherwise dull trip. It was well known, however, that Captain Joseph Skeldon of the *Dows* had bragged that he could cross Lake Erie by daylight, which was no easy task, and this may have added a bit more intensity to the competition. In any event, the race ended when a quick shift in wind direction left all three captains fighting for control of their vessels. The *Dows* ended up ramming the *Nims*, which sank almost immediately. No lives were lost, but the ensuing investigation into the incident left the captains of these vessels with tarnished records.

The *Dows* was to meet her end on Thanksgiving Day, 1889. The Great Lakes experience some of their worst weather conditions in November when high winds and turbulent seas combine with cold temperatures, rain, sleet or driving snow. At the time of her sinking, the *Dows* carried a full load of coal from Erie, PA, to Chicago under tow of the steamship *Aurora*. In stormy waters just south of Chicago's

Calumet Harbor, the *Dows* began taking on water into her holds at an alarming rate and her bilge pumps were put to work. The amount of water the ship was taking on, however, continued to increase and the *Aurora* cut the towing line between the two vessels in hopes of easing the strain on the *Dows* and cutting down on the amount of water she was taking on. The tactic worked for a while as water inside the vessel was held at bay until

the pumps malfunctioned. The crew waited for help and eventually the tug *Cromwell* arrived and rescued the men on board *Dows*. Apparently, this was just in the nick of time for after the evacuation the waterlogged *Dows* reportedly rolled over and sank, settling upright on the floor of Lake Michigan with all five of her masts sticking up through the surface of the water. An investigation was carried out to determine whether it would be

worth the effort to raise the ship, but the damage was too great and what remains of the *Dows* today rests where she went down in 1889.

## The *Eastland* Disaster

One of the greatest maritime tragedies in Great Lakes history occurred, oddly enough, at dockside in the narrow channel of the Chicago River. It was here that the *Eastland* disaster took place on July 24, 1915.

The five-masted schooner *David Dows* in tow by the tugboat *Winslow*, 1882.
Graphic courtesy of the Dossin Museum of Great Lakes History

Passenger liner *Eastland*, overturned at dockside in Chicago Harbor, 1915. The death of over 800 people makes this tragedy the worst in Great Lakes maritime history. Photo courtesy of the Chicago Maritime Society

*Eastland* was a narrow and tall ship 265 feet long and weighing 1900 tons. She was built for fuel efficiency and speed as a lake freighter, but with three decks she was also suited for passenger excursions that frequently took place during summer months.

Reportedly, *Eastland* was difficult to handle with a greater than normal tendency to list from one side to the other but the ship was seaworthy when handled properly.

On the morning of July 24, 1915, Eastland was tied at the dock to receive an estimated 2,500 employees of the Western Electric Company who were taking a holiday trip across Lake Michigan. The passengers began crowding aboard at 7:00 a.m. when the ship began to sway toward the dock. Only half the load of Western Electric workers had boarded, so the chief engineer simply balanced the vessel by letting water into the ballast tanks. Passengers continued to stream onto the ship until, with some 2,500 people on board, the gangplanks were drawn up and the order given to start the engines. Then, *Eastland* suddenly tilted toward the river causing panic among the passengers who lost their balance as the captain tried to steer the ship into the river channel.

*"The Eastland was already to pull out, when suddenly she went over on her side, and then there were horrible things happening. I heard women screaming and shrieking and children crying out and everybody seemed mad. It seemed to take the big boat only a few seconds to turn over on its side."*

Mildred Anderson, *Chicago Daily News*, July 25, 1915

There was only a brief pause between the time *Eastland* tilted toward the river and finally rolled over, her starboard side hitting river bottom. Those people on deck who hadn't been thrown into the river by the force of the motion began to jump overboard for their own safety. Bystanders rescued many people afloat, but the river current and panic took many lives. A more grisly scene was played out below deck, where many more passengers drowned as water rushed into the hull. In all, 815 people died in this tragedy.

Responsibility for the accident was never determined. Critics charged that *Eastland* turned over because she carried too many passengers and yet the number of passengers on board was within her registered limits. The Steamboat Inspection Service could only conclude that no one was at fault. The organization fell under the Department of Commerce and it was Secretary William Redfield's personal belief that the ship's design contributed to the lack of stability that eventually led to the accident.

Unlike her drowned passengers, *Eastland* received a second life as a naval training ship named the *Wilmette*.

### Flora M. Hill

The sinking of *Flora M. Hill* is an example of just how destructive ice can be on the Great Lakes and elsewhere. The *Hill* was originally christened in 1874 as the lighthouse tender *Dahlia* carrying fuel, food and other supplies to lighthouses on the Great Lakes. She was 130 feet in length, some 26 feet across at her widest point, and had a draft of 20 feet. A propeller steamer, the *Dahlia* was the first tender specifically designed for working the Great Lakes and was also the first ship of her kind to have an iron hull. She operated effectively for the Lighthouse Service for 35 years before being sold to the Hill steamboat line of Kenosha, WI, in 1909. Hill engineers modified the ship and installed heavy metal plating on the hull for navigation through ice in winter months. Renamed *Flora M. Hill*, the vessel went into the freight trade between Chicago and Milwaukee.

The *Hill* departed Kenosha, WI, on March 10, 1912 with her heaviest cargo of the season, comprised of brass beds and automobile running lamps. Travel time was extended because of wintery conditions but the vessel slowly plodded along the shipping lane towards Chicago until becoming trapped in ice over a mile from Chicago's two-mile water crib just outside of the harbor entrance. The keeper of Chicago's crib saw the ship at daylight lying low in the water and flying its distress signal. A total of 32 people, including the captain, crew, and passengers, abandoned the ship in an effort to reach the crib. Their trip to safety was treacherous and took the group over an hour as they walked toward the crib, dodging life-threatening crevices in the ice. The captain, W.E. Hill, later recounted that he had steered the ship along the edge of the ice pack and expected to make Chicago River without incident when a big cake of ice was forced under the boat near the crib. The force of the impact was so great that it

Lighthouse tender *Dahlia*. During the early years of lighthouse administration under the Lighthouse Board of 1852, vessels were chartered to deliver supplies to lights on the Great Lakes. This changed, however, in 1857 when it was decided to purchase and staff ships as part of light tending operations. Built in 1874, the *Dahlia* was a propeller steamer and the first iron-hulled tender designed exclusively for work on the Great Lakes. Interestingly, her christening marked the beginning of naming subsequent lighthouse tenders after plants, flowers, and trees. In addition to the *Dahlia,* the tenders *Marigold* and *Amaranth* are but two other examples of this practice. The building in the background is a lighthouse supply depot located in Detroit. Completed in 1874, this facility was the first one on the Great Lakes and was constructed to store fuel, lenses, and other items necessary to maintain lighthouses.
Photo courtesy of the Milwaukee Public Library, Humanities Collections

Steamship *Flora Hill* at dockside. After structural modifications were done in 1909, she bears little resemblance to her former existence as the *Dahlia,* pictured at left. Photo courtesy of the Milwaukee Public Library, Humanities Collections

lifted part of the ship out of the water and punched a hole in its bottom. The flow of water into the vessel was more than the bilge pumps could handle and a call for aid was sent into Chicago. Despite the lake ice, a virtual flotilla of salvage ships arrived only to see the *Flora E. Hill* settle in 35 feet of water, her iron hull plates–supposed protection against ice–scattered on the lake bottom.

## The Tragedy of *Favorite*

*Favorite* was a wooden, open, double-decked passenger boat 57 feet long and was typical of those that roamed the waters close to Chicago up until the latter part of the 1920s. Powered by a small single-cylinder gas engine, *Favorite* transported passengers between Chicago's Lincoln Park landing and Municipal (Navy) Pier, about two miles away. This vessel was constructed in 1914 and took advantage of the popular excursion boat business of the period. The ship changed owners several times before finally ending up in the hands of one Arthur "Beef" Olson, a prominent local boat captain and a professional masseur to boot. The tragedy of *Favorite* began to unfold during the afternoon of Thursday, July 28, 1927. With 62 passengers on board, Captain Olson and a crew of five steered the ship from its loading area at 3:30 p.m for what was supposed to be a pleasant trip along Chicago's waterfront. After some time, *Favorite* began to encounter increasingly stiff southwesterly winds that were blowing menacing looking clouds over the city and the ship was soon in the grip of a gale-force storm that seemed to come out of nowhere very quickly. Olson fought to maintain control of his craft but could not and the vessel began to turn broadside to the wind and waves as the intensity of the sudden squall increased. The rapid movement of passengers away from the elements tipped the boat so that the blustery wind caught the canvas awning on the top deck and turned the vessel into the water. Passengers on the upper deck were swept off by the high waves and those on the lower deck were carried down with the boat. *Favorite* eventually settled on the lake bottom with its pilothouse above relatively shallow water.

Rescue efforts were begun immediately with police boats, tugs, Coast Guard craft and private vessels lending a hand to aid passengers who had been thrown into the water and those stranded below deck, but 27 lives were lost. There were no less than four separate inquiries into this disaster but the verdict attributed the accident to an unfortunate act of nature, possibly made worse by the instability of the boat when the passengers shifted position. In fact, the ship was surveyed by the Steamboat Inspection Service just 16 days prior to the accident and found to be in good condition. Nearly four years after the accident, *Favorite* was sold and eventually returned to service along Chicago's lakefront as an excursion vessel named the *Sunbeam*. But by 1937, the wooden hull of the ship was badly deteriorating and the vessel was finally scrapped.

The excursion boat *Favorite,* was rescued from the spot where she went beneath the waves off Chicago's waterfront and brought back to port for inspection. There were 27 deaths as a result of this tragedy. Photo courtesy of the Chicago Historical Society

## The U.S. Life–Saving Service

Despite the best efforts of the federal government and the Lighthouse Service in marking the way into port, shipwrecks still occurred in and around Chicago's Harbor. In an effort to add an extra dimension of safety, the federal government created a United States Life–Saving Service for the purpose of rescuing victims of coastal sea disasters. It was the only governmental unit of its kind in the world and complemented aids to navigation in helping to ensure that ships, cargoes, passengers and crew would reach port. The Life–Saving Service had its origins in 1807 but it was not formally established until 1878 when it became an agency within the Treasury Department under the supervision of Sumner I. Kimball, General Superintendent. Kimball was, in fact, the only superintendent the Service ever had and held reign over the organization until it was merged with the U.S. Coast Guard in 1915.

Life saving stations were constructed around coasts and shores where there would be heavy ship traffic. The first stations were designed as simple single-story structures, but by the 1880s it was common for buildings to have 2-3 floors with a lookout tower on the roof. Some life-saving stations were comprised of multiple buildings that would be used for offices, boathouse, and quarters for the crew. On the Great Lakes, most stations took the form of two–story buildings. The surfboat served as their

Chicago.
U. S. Life Boat Station.

B. Sebastian, Publisher, Chicago.

The U.S. Life–Saving Station in Chicago, ca.1878.
Nancy Osika Post Card Collection.

main rescue craft and was kept on the first floor of the building with other necessary aids such as sand anchors, hawsers and mortars for shooting lines across stranded vessels. The second floor offered living quarters for a keeper, the crew and victims of maritime disasters. A crewman's service on the Great Lakes normally spanned eight months and paralleled the weather-shortened shipping season there. Initially, crewman could be no more than 45 years of age, but there was no retirement system and salaries were too low to attract new men. As a result, shortly before the merger of the Service and U.S. Coast Guard there were instances of men in their 60s and 70s who worked as oarmen in the surfboats. At the height of operation of the Service in 1890, there were 18 life saving stations on Lake Michigan and two of these—one in suburban Evanston and the other at the mouth of the Chicago river—served water-borne transportation using Chicago's harbor.

The Chicago Harbor Life-Saving Station was built in 1876 on the south bank of the Chicago River. At first, this structure served only as a boat-house to complement the fully staffed life saving station in Evanston, 12 miles north. However, a full service station was built on a breakwater at the mouth to the Chicago River in 1903 and was operational for 30 years. In 1936, a third life-saving station was constructed at the south end of the harbor entrance by the U.S. Coast Guard. During its years of existence before absorption into the Coast Guard, Chicago Harbor's Life–Saving Station helped 359 ships in distress.

The two principal methods of rescue practiced by the Service were to use a surfboat with crew or by sending a strong line from the beach to the wrecked vessel for assistance. The Life-Saving Service's surfboats were legendary because of their effectiveness in maneuvering through turbulent water to get to their goal. In addition to using a surfboat when a ship was wrecked close to shore a strong hawser, or heavy rope line, would be sent to the ship by using the "Lyle" gun that looked like a small cannon. This gun could propel a safety line up to 600 yards to a ship in distress. When the line was secure, a "life car" was pulled back and forth between the vessel and land bringing people to safety. The life car looked like a small submarine with a watertight hatch for entry and exit, and it typically carried four to six people. Of course, all of the equipment meant nothing without a good life saving crew and the rescues performed by the men of the U.S. Life-Saving Service captured the

John Conlon of the U.S. Life-Saving Service crew in Chicago, ca. 1906. The men who made up the crews, known as surfmen, could initially be no more than 45 years of age and the number of men comprised a crew at most stations was determined by the number of oars needed to pull the largest boat–usually six to eight. Although, at busy harbors like Chicago, crews might consist of up to 10 individuals. Mr. Conlon is seen here wearing a medal for exceptional valor in the line of duty. In fact, the heroic efforts of the life saving crews gave rise to their being described by the press as "soldiers of the surf" and "storm warriors."
Photos courtesy of the Chicago Historical Society

The Life–Saving Service frequently practiced their rescue skills in order to remain sharp in emergency situations. This photo documents a life saving crew launching their heavy surf-boat into the frigid waters of Lake Michigan during a training drill.

Every Tuesday, the life saving crew was required to practice launching and landing their boats in the surf, capsizing them in the water, and then turning them right side up again. On Monday's and Thursday's, the crew could be seen practicing maneuvers that might be required for saving lives on board a ship that had wrecked near shore. The entire drill had to be completed in five minutes and at times would be supervised by a USLSS District Inspector who would dismiss from the service any crewman he thought was moving too slowly. Practice in signaling and first aid was required of each crewman and beach patrol and lookout duties were other important aspects of a crewman's job.

attention of the public for better and sometimes for worse.

A difficult job under any circumstances, the Service was sometimes subject to adverse scrutiny by the press. The October 14, 1893 edition of the *Chicago Tribune* told of a series of maritime disasters due to a heavy fog that had descended over Lake Michigan for the greater part of two days. The article went on to describe a life and death situation, commenting that "the life saving crew... was about as useful as if they had been in some other state." The loss of the schooner *Myrtle* during a fierce storm on May 18, 1894 also placed the Chicago Life Saving Crew under public scrutiny and much of what was said about their rescue attempts in the daily newspapers was not flattering, with charges of drunkenness and ineptitude. The *Myrtle* lost seven of her crew as she sank and an irate press wanted to know why. A formal investigation by the U.S. Life-Saving Service, however, failed to lay the blame on the crew. On the day of the tragedy they had responded to eight calls for help and made the best effort possible to save the *Myrtle* and her crew in their exhausted physical condition.

Despite these lackluster appraisals of Chicago's Life–Saving Service crews, records indicate that they saved almost 98 percent of the lives endangered on their rescue missions and 85 percent of the property at risk (Grossman & Karamanski, 1989). In the end, the history of the U.S. Life-Saving Service at Chicago is one of both heroism and exemplary commitment to duty.

Post card view of the U.S. Life–Saving Station in Chicago, ca.1909.
Nancy Osika Post Card Collection

Captain Charles Carland of the Chicago Life-Saving Station is shown here dressed in the characteristic oilskin coat and hat that proved to be an effective barrier to the cold damp environment in which crews worked.
Photo ca. 1911 Photo courtesy of the Chicago Historical Society

# Chicago's Harbor Lights

Two views of the original 1832 Chicago Harbor Lighthouse. The illustration at left is from Andreas' *History of Chicago* (1894) and depicts the lighthouse in close proximity to Fort Dearborn's (1816) stockade. The view above is from a rare albumen print ca. 1850 and shows the top half of the lighthouse sticking up among the buildings of Fort Dearborn. Like many lighthouses of the time, the light tower was constructed of rubble stone that most likely was found in the immediate vicinity. The lantern exhibits the so-called "birdcage" design that was found in association with the Lewis lighting system, consisting of oil lamps and large reflector panels. This lighthouse design was used infrequently on the Great Lakes but an example still exists in the form of Old Bailey's Harbor Light in Bailey's Harbor, WI. Photo courtesy of the Chicago Historical Society.

Mention the word lighthouse to the average person and the image of a tall masonry tower standing on shore near the water comes to mind. Actually, lighthouses come in many shapes and sizes and are made of wood, stone, brick, reinforced concrete, iron, steel and other materials. They are built on land, in the water, on small islands, breakwaters, and at the end of piers. In fact, lighthouses are a form of technology and like all types of technology evolve and develop in order to fill a respective need. The current Chicago Harbor lighthouse is the last link in a chain of lighthouses and other navigational aids that have served the city's port since 1832. Interestingly, Chicago's lighthouses represent a variety of structural types. Architecturally, each of these was distinctly different from the others and represents a broad cross-section of

lighthouse design. They all, however, were placed in operation because of the need to help ships navigate safely through the waters surrounding one of the world's great inland city ports.

The history of lighting Chicago's Harbor begins on March 3, 1831 when Congress approved the expenditure of $5,000 for building a lighthouse at the mouth to the Chicago River. There is little documentation left regarding this lighthouse, but an interesting account is related by A.T. Andreas in The History of Chicago, published in 1884.

> During March 1831, after the United States engineers had suggested a plan for the improvement of the harbor, an appropriation of $5,000 was obtained for the erection of a lighthouse. Before it was fairly completed, however, on October 30 of that year, the structure fell. A few hours before it toppled over, so confident were

many there was no danger of its falling, that several went upon the top of it, some of the visitors being women. The walls were three feet thick, and the tower had to be raised to a height of fifty feet. Samual Jackson was the contractor. He claimed that the lighthouse had been built on quicksand, which caused the building to settle and fall; others held that the cause was the defective manner in which it was built. Another tower, forty feet high, was begun and completed by Mr. Jackson in 1832.

Another interesting statement was published in 1834 by J.M. Peck in his *Gazetteer of Illinois* that makes reference to Chicago's "lighthouses" as if there were more than one. Mr. Andreas' source for the information published in his book is not mentioned and apparently has slipped away over the years. And the statement by Mr. Peck referring to more than one lighthouse being present in

Illustration depicting the 1832 Chicago Harbor Lighthouse and Chicago River. From a watercolor painting by Justin Herriott. Photo courtesy of the Chicago Historical Society

Old Bailey's Harbor Lighthouse, Wisconsin, was built in 1852 and its tower bears a striking resemblance to Chicago's first lighthouse of 1832. Photo courtesy of Wayne Sapulski

1832 presents us with conflicting reports that are difficult to interpret. In addition, seemingly contradictory documentation exists in the Lighthouse Board's General Correspondence Files where there is a letter dated June 6, 1881, from Commander George Dewey, Naval Secretary, addressed to Mr. John Wentworth of the Chicago Historical Society.

Your letter of May 27, relative to the old Chicago Lighthouse, within the precincts of Fort Dearborn, has been received.

In reply I have to say that the structure in question was built, served its purpose, was discontinued and removed prior to the organization of the Light-House Board [1852], and that the only

information this office can obtain with regard to it is from the imperfect records which have come down from those who from time to time previously had charge of the light-house service. Such of the information which you ask as the board is able to furnish is herein given.

The records of the office show nothing with regard to the tradition you mention relative to the destruction of a light-house in 1831 and the erection of a new one on the same spot. There appears, thus far, no evidence that there was any light-house at Fort Dearborn prior to 1831…It appears from the various lighthouse lists that were published by the Treasury Department from 1838 to 1857 that the Chicago light-house was erected in 1831-2, but the precise date upon which it was commenced and upon which it was finished is not given.

An earlier letter from the Light-House Board to the Secretary of the Treasury dated April 11, 1878, can only make reference to a lighthouse being built at Chicago "before the 1st day of May 1834." These sources raise considerable doubt about exactly what happened, presenting a somewhat controversial beginning to the history of lighting the important Port of Chicago. At any rate, what we do know about the first documented lighthouse is that it was completed sometime in 1832 on the south side of the Chicago River not far from the stockade of Fort Dearborn. The fort was named after Henry Dearborn, Secretary of War in Thomas Jefferson's presidential cabinet. For people interested in the history of lighthouses, it's of note that Henry Dearborn also

Drawing of Fort Dearborn and Chicago Harbor Lighthouse of 1832. Photo courtesy of the Chicago Historical Society

1832 Chicago Harbor Lighthouse after the great flood of 1849 had left many schooners stranded on the Chicago River banks. Illustration from Andreas, 1884

built the first light tower to mark Cape Hatteras in North Carolina.

In the Treasury Department's lighthouse list for 1838, the tower at Chicago is described as a masonry structure, 40 feet in height. Early depictions of this structure show it to be constructed of rubble stone, probably obtained locally. The lantern on the structure appears to have been one of the rare so-called "birdcage" designs that was occasionally used with the early Argand lighting system. It emitted a fixed white light through the use of four 14-inch parabolic reflectors, each of which were fitted with an oil-burning lamp. This lighting system was common for the time and was invented by Winslow Lewis, a civilian who profited greatly from its use by the federal government. The 1832 Chicago Lighthouse was the first constructed on Lake Michigan, followed closely by a light at St. Joseph, Michigan.

While formally ushering in Chicago's age of shipping, the lighthouse of 1832 was of limited navigational use because it's location was too far inland. As a result, ships had difficulty spotting the light and finding the river's entrance – at times becoming stranded on a sand bar. This brief report by Lieutenant G.J. Pendergrast, U.S. Navy, to Commodore Chauncey, President of the Board of Navy Commissioners, was written on Aug. 18, 1837 and is on file at the National Archives in Documents Relating to Lighthouses, 1789-1871.

Chicago is situated about sixty-five miles south of Root River. This is a highly important place, containing about six thousand inhabitants. There is a good stationary light here, and a harbor nearly completed. It now forms the only place of shelter along the entire western shore of Lake Michigan, and has already been the means of saving many lives and much property. When the piers are finished, the light house ought to be placed on one of them, and the old light should then be discontinued.

Indeed, the construction of piers into Lake Michigan and harbor dredging activities created easier access to the river port but also brought about the need to place a beacon light at the end of the pier in 1847. Continued expansion of harbor facilities eventually created the need for a new lighthouse. According to the Lighthouse Board's Annual Report, on March 3, 1849, Congress appropriated $15,000 for *"the foundation and construction of a lighthouse at or near the end of North Pier at Chicago, to be expended under direction of the Bureau of Topographical Engineers, and the present [1832] lighthouse within the city, and the beacon light on the pier, shall be discontinued from and after completion of the aforesaid lighthouse."* This appropriation was the first in a long series of others that spanned a decade before the new lighthouse was commissioned in 1859.

Part of the problem with completing this project in a timely manner arose because of government investigations into the ineffectiveness of Stephen Pleasonton's leadership

Chicago's 1859 lighthouse being disassembled in 1894. The lantern and some other minor parts of the structure were used in the construction of Rawley Point Lighthouse near Twin Rivers, Wisconsin.
U.S. Coast Guard photo

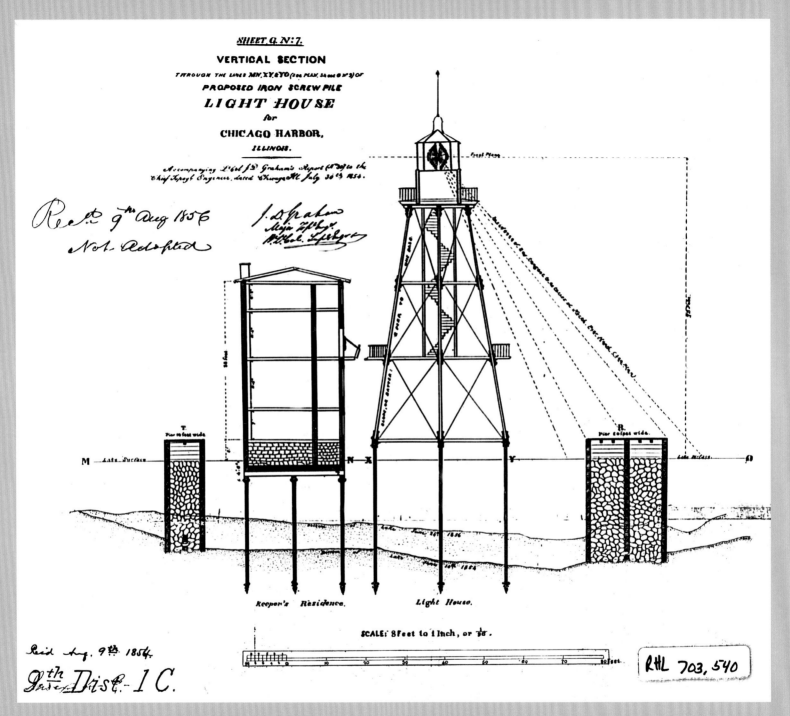

Architectural plans for the 1859 Chicago Harbor Lighthouse. This lighthouse had a much different look than its predecessor for instead of stone, the lantern at the top rested on iron supports that created a so-called skeleton tower. This was a less expensive type of construction, but the original idea behind the design was that it did not form as much of an obstacle to the natural elements as a large masonry structure. The stilt-like support columns and the overall design was the invention of Englishman Henry Whiteside, who successfully used this type of lighthouse for the first time in constructing the Smalls Reef Lighthouse in 1774 off the west coast of Britain. Illustration from the National Archives

within the Department of the Treasury. There was particularly harsh criticism for the manner in which the department handled business relating to the construction and administration of aids to navigation. As a result, responsibility for lighthouses and other navigational aids was eventually transferred in 1852 to a Lighthouse Board comprised of individuals representing a cross-section of government agencies and civilian scientists. Working in this environment of government investigations and imminent administrative changes must surely have been difficult for those involved with the Chicago project, resulting in delayed decisions to appropriate money or award construction contracts.

On March 3, 1851, $4,498.39 was appropriated for completing the foundation and construction of the lighthouse at the end of North Pier. This was followed by $6,300 on Aug. 31, 1852. In 1853, the Annual Report of the Lighthouse Board to Congress indicated that the pierhead put down for the foundation of the lighthouse was sufficient for the purpose for which it was designed, and that *"the light should be one of the first class for the lakes which is the equivalent to a third order lens. This lens . . . is very much needed, as the present one is very imperfect and altogether insufficient. I think that eventually it would be a saving to the government to construct an iron beacon on the end of north pier, in place of the frail structure in present use."*

Planning for this new lighthouse came in the nick of time, as it was reported in a communication between Inspector G.H. Scott and the Eleventh Lighthouse District headquarters in Detroit on August 26, 1857, that the old Chicago Lighthouse built in 1832 was cracked and in danger of falling down. The recommendation for a new light was made by Lieutenant Webster of the Corps of Topographical Engineers and was eventually accepted by the Lighthouse Board. Supervising the construction of this lighthouse fell to Major J.D. Graham, Superintending Engineer. The iron-work for the structure was completed in 1857, and the erection of the lighthouse began during the spring of 1858. The construction of the keepers' quarters and protective cribs for the lighthouse foundation were also underway, and it was reported in the Lighthouse Board's Annual Report for 1857 that *"The materials have all been collected for the completion of the work, and the board is informed by the engineer that the structure will be finished and ready for lighting by the end of August, 1858."* Bad weather delayed completion of the project until it was finally lighted and began formal operation on July 9, 1859.

An interesting bit of intrigue emerged in association with the establishment of this new light. The Lighthouse Board's Correspondence File Index indicates that the light-house was turned over to G.H. Scott, District Inspector at this time, who recommended that the lighthouse keeper, Mark Beaubien, should be

Illustration of Chicago's 1859 lighthouse from the *Chicago Inter-Ocean*, November 9, 1890.

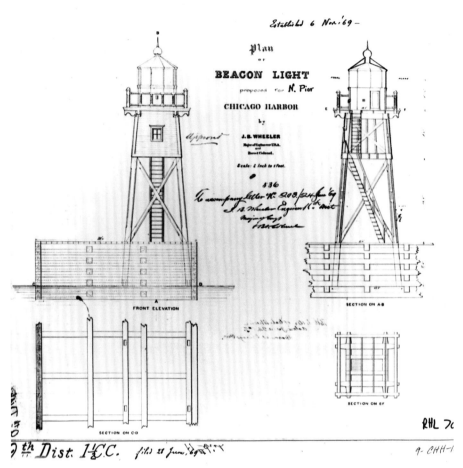

Design for the Chicago Harbor North Pier Beacon Light, constructed in 1869.
Illustration from the National Archives

1859, is eighty-three feet above lake level, and is visible sixteen miles. This is the principal one of seven lights maintained by the government as aids to navigation near the mouth of the Chicago River. The harbor here is the most important on the lakes, with a greater average number of daily arrivals and departures during the season of navigation than any other in the United States. This city is in the ninth lighthouse district. The eleventh district formerly embraced the three Great Lakes-Michigan, Huron and up to the National line of Superior. The ninth is a division of the eleventh district. It includes all aids to navigation on Lake Michigan, Green Bay and tributary waters lying west of a line drawn across the Straits of Mackinac at the narrowest part east of McGulpin's Point light station.

Captain Ole Hansen is principal keeper at Chicago light, and has a first and second assistant. Simon P. Nelson is first, and Edward N. Curran is second assistant light-keeper. Captain Hansen and his family reside in the substantial two-story frame just west of the lighthouse.

Expansion of Chicago's Harbor facilities continued and, in 1865, North Pier was extended 450 feet into Lake Michigan. A small beacon light was constructed at the end of the pier to aid navigation into harbor. This required an appropriation of $3,000 from Congress made on July 28, 1866. Construction of the beacon was completed in 1869 and it was fitted with a sixth-order Fresnel lens for magnification of the light.

At this point in time, the government finally realized that North Pier was going to need to be lengthened

once again and the Lighthouse Board commented in its Annual Report for 1869 that *"The extension of the piers at this point may require a removal of the light to another position at a not so very distant day."* Indeed, when the 1859 lighthouse was built it marked the extreme end of North Pier. By 1870, the pier had been extended into Lake Michigan an additional 1,200 feet from the lighthouse. Furthermore, the smoke from steamships and Chicago's many factories along the river obscured this light. In recognition of these factors, the Lighthouse Board recommended that the main guiding light into Chicago should be moved to a more suitable location some 12 miles north on a promontory of land called Grosse Point in suburban Evanston. It was also recommended that the wooden dwelling remain and serve as a home for the keeper of the beacon and *"From its gable end a light to be shown which, with the beacon, will form a range indicating the direction of the North Harbor pier."* So, Chicago's lights became officially known as the Chicago River (main) Light and pierhead light. By 1874, the lake coastal light at Grosse Point had been completed and worked effectively with the two Chicago Harbor lights in getting lake traffic safely in and out of port and back into the shipping lanes. By 1880, however, the foundation for the iron-framed Chicago River Light needed to be reconstructed at a cost of $10,000 and by 1886 a new open-frame tower was built to replace the old one at the pier

relieved of his position on charges of neglect of duty and incapacity to perform the job. Mr. Beaubien unexpectedly resigned on short notice and in an apparent cry for help Inspector Scott–unfamiliar with how to operate the Fresnel optical apparatus–requested instructions as to lighting of the beacon and added that the appointment of a new keeper as soon as possible was highly recommended. Whatever infraction caused keeper Beaubien to resign resulted in the

sudden transfer of responsibilities to Mr. Scott. Some years later, a feature article titled "Our Coast Beacons" was published in the Sunday issue of the *Chicago Inter-Ocean*, November 9, 1890 and contains the following description of the 1859 structure:

> Chicago light is a third-order fixed white light in a black, skeleton iron tower, with stair cylinder, connected by covered way with the keepers dwelling. It is located on the inner pier, north side of the Chicago River; was established in

Augustin Jean Fresnel (1788-1827) inventor of the Fresnel Lens Optical System. Prior to Fresnel's invention, the source of illumination used in American lighthouses was from multiple oil lamps fitted with highly polished metal reflectors. Much of the radiant light emitted from this arrangement was lost and lighthouses using the technology were never very effective or efficient. In contrast, Fresnel's illuminating apparatus was based on using the refractive and magnifying properties of glass prisms to capture and intensify the light coming from a single lamp inside the lens as it was projected from the lighthouse lantern. The Fresnel lens came in various sizes or "orders" from one (the largest) to six. This highly effective lens configuration could cast a beam of light from a first-order lens over more than 20 miles of open water in good atmospheric conditions. Photo by D.J. Terras

Fifth-order Fresnel lens in Lighthouse Service depot workshop. Photo from the National Archives

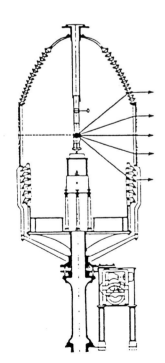
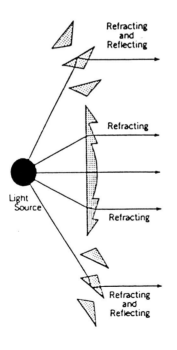

The glass prisms from a Fresnel lens capture the radiant light coming from an oil lamp and concentrate it as the beacon is emitted from the lighthouse lantern. Illustration from the U.S. Coast Guard

head. Then, in 1889, the Lighthouse Board proposed that a new light station should be constructed at the end of a breakwater away from the ship traffic immediately in and around North Pier. Its placement would make the light a much more effective navigational aid, directing lake traffic into the harbor area where a ship's position could then be determined by using minor lights on the piers and shoreline of the river itself.

*"The harbor of Chicago is the most important on the lakes, with a greater average number of daily arrivals and departures during the season of navigation than any other in the United States."* This statement appeared in the Annual Report of the Lighthouse Board in 1889 and was made in defense of the proposal for a new Chicago Harbor Light. It underscores how commercial interests in the Midwest were tied to Chicago's inland port facility and recognition of the need to better mark the port entrance. In response, an appropriation of $36,000 was made for construction of a new light station. The Lighthouse Board's General Correspondence Files contain a letter dated April 29, 1889, with a cost breakdown for the new structure:

Foundation-crib: $230.60
Superstructure of crib: $8,604.60
Iron tower: $12,578.00
Fog-signals and house: $4,603.54
2 iron boat cranes: $500.00
Tank for water supply: $300.00
Foot bridge: $183.26
Contingencies: $3,000.00
Total: $36,000.00

This total amount was found to be insufficient, however, and an

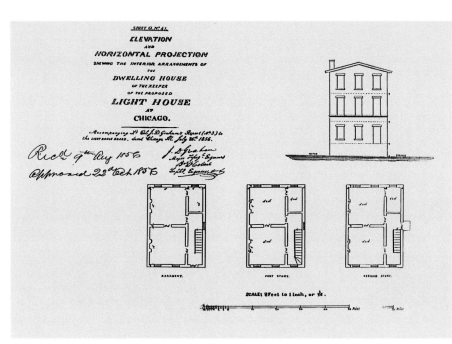

The design of the keepers' quarters for the 1859 Chicago lighthouse included a retractable walkway connecting the tower to the house. Plans from National Archives

After the 1859 lighthouse was decommissioned and disassembled in 1894, the keepers' quarters building was structurally modified and used as an office for the U.S. Lighthouse Service in Chicago. Photo from the National Archives

additional $15,000 was requested from Congress. *"The [initial] amount of appropriation is quite inadequate for the purpose, admitting only of building a perishable and unsightly wooden crib with a plain iron tower upon it. The woodwork should be replaced with stone, and the tower, occupying so prominent a place in port, should have some pretensions to architectural effect."* – Annual Report of the Lighthouse Board, 1889.

The total of $51,000 still did not seem to satisfy the Lighthouse Board, who commented in its Annual Report to Congress in 1891 that it was a *"small enough sum considering that the light will be the leading one in the most important harbor on the lakes, and the act requiring its construction on an independent crib site two miles from shore, and to include a fog signal also."*

Major William Ludlow, Ninth Lighthouse District Engineer at the time, summed up the situation: *"It is submitted that in a case of a harbor so important and thronged as that of Chicago, and of a station to be built in so conspicuous a position, it would be both a false economy and a disparagement of the government work to construct it otherwise than in the best manner and of the best and most enduring materials."* – Letter to Lighthouse Board dated April 13, 1889. General Correspondence Files, National Archives.

Work on the foundation of the crib that would support the light

station was finally started on September 25, 1889 and the crib was put into position on December 25th of that year. The structure was 40 feet by 60 feet in plan and 23 feet high. and was loaded with 287 cords of stone, and rested on a base of riprap 10 feet in thickness. Plans and specifications for the tower were made and in May of 1891 proposals were sought and a construction contract made. However, owing to delays in obtaining the steel casing connecting the crib foundation with the stone superstructure, the foundation was not fully completed until May of 1892. All drain and soil pipes and cistern and cellar curbs were located and the crib was then filled with concrete. A Congressional Act of March 3, 1893, appropriated $15,500 more for completing construction of this station. This included an additional 694 cords of riprap stone on the southeast, southwest and northwest sides. The mechanical device that rotated the Fresnel lens optic was paid for with $4,300 of this money and two fog signal houses were erected, one on either side of the light tower. Each house was 11 feet by 24 feet in plan, 12 feet high and constructed of heavy framing lumber covered with a two-inch planking. The exterior was sheathed with corrugated iron, both on the sides and roof.

The station was provided with duplicate ten-inch steam whistles. The Russel Wheel & Foundry Company

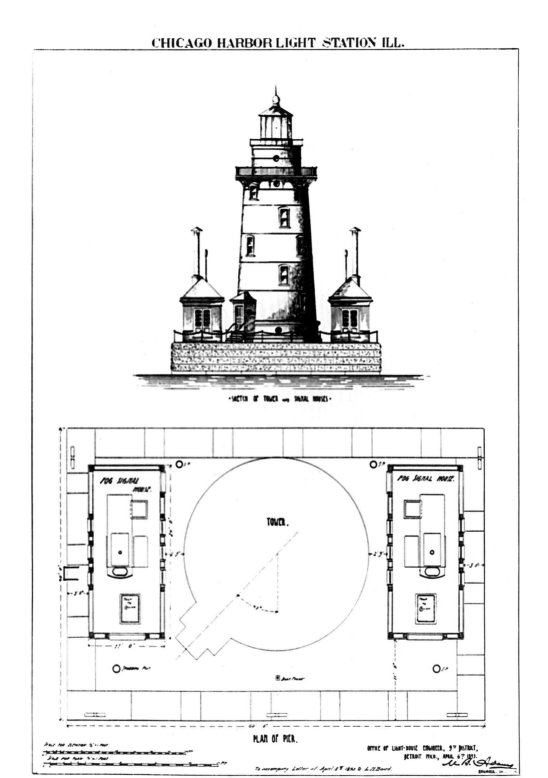

·SECTION OF TOWER and SIGNAL HOUSES·

FOG SIGNAL HOUSE.        FOG SIGNAL HOUSE.

TOWER.

PLAN OF PIER.

OFFICE OF LIGHT-HOUSE ENGINEER, 9TH DISTRICT,
DETROIT MICH., APRIL 6TH 1893.

To accompany Letter of April 8th 1893 to L.H.Board.

Architectural detail of the 1893 Chicago Harbor Light Station. Plans from the National Archives

completed construction of the light tower on September 1, 1893. In a communication contained in the Lighthouse Board's General Correspondence Files, John J. Brice, Ninth District Inspector, wrote on October 2, 1893 that *"I have the honor to call the board's attention to the establishment of the Chicago Harbor Lighthouse, which will be completed in about one month."*

Brice was perhaps feeling some pressure for this project to be wrapped up and, true to his word, this light was exhibited for the first time on the night of November 9, 1893. As it turned out, this happened none to soon. "City Lost In The Mists"... "About the Worst Fog That Was Ever Known Here Ingulfs Chicago" reads the headline for a column in the *Chicago Daily News* on the date the light was first lit. Recognizing the danger to Chicago's harbor traffic, it was reported in the November 11, 1893, *Chicago Inter-Ocean* that District Inspector Brice also ordered the operation of the new fog signal on the south end of the exterior breakwater nearly a week earlier than anticipated, doubtlessly because of the unusually poor atmospheric conditions during this time.

Completion of the 1893 light station made keeping track of all Chicago's lights a bit more complicated. The latest addition was dubbed the Chicago Harbor Light, which went along with the Chicago River Light and Chicago Pierhead Range Lights.

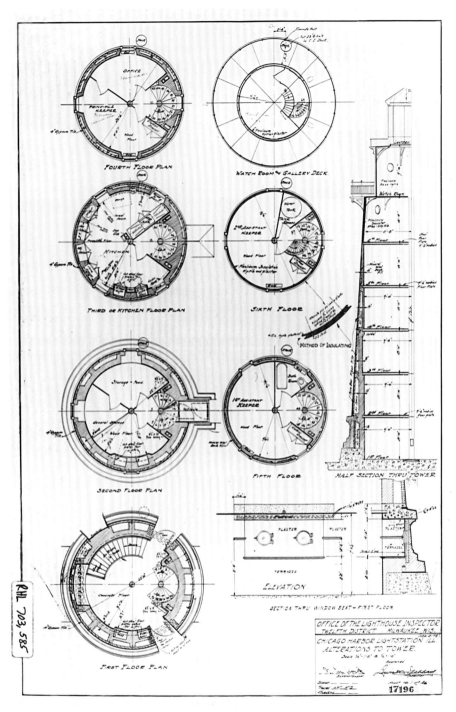

Architectural cross-section of the 1893 Chicago Harbor lighthouse showing the floor plan of the light tower. Plans from the National Archives

In addition, another lighthouse had been constructed on a water intake crib for the City of Chicago and by 1890, there were lights at the ends of two outer breakwaters constructed to protect the submarine foundations of piers and other commercial shipping structures in and around what came to be formally called the Chicago Harbor of Refuge. However, the Lighthouse Board had plans for the river light. On October 25, 1893, District Inspector Brice recommended discontinuance of the third-order fixed white light at Chicago River Light Station. He further recommended that the Chicago River reservation be used as a storage place for buoys and appendages and that the keepers dwelling continue to be used by the Lighthouse Service for offices and living quarters for a principal keeper. Action regarding this matter was taken on October 31 of the same year when the Location Committee of the Lighthouse Establishment went even further in stating that *"it has been decided to take down the tower at the discontinued Chicago River, Illinois, light-station, and to have it re-erected at the Twin River, Wisconsin, light station."* The Engineer Secretary of the Lighthouse Board finally gave his approval on April 16, 1894 and the project began. The illuminating apparatus was taken down, packed and boxed, shipped to Detroit and stored at the lighthouse depot located there. Measurements of the Chicago

tower and sketches of the lantern were made with a view to making alterations and additions for use at Twin River Point (now known as Rawley Point). The work of taking down the skeleton iron tower commenced on June 7, 1894 and by the end of the month, all of the structure had been taken down to the top of the lower story. Nearly all of the small parts were invoiced and boxed and other parts bundled for shipment. This extensive inventory aside, the primary watchroom and lantern were the only parts from Chicago destined for use at Twin River Point Light Station.

By 1906, the War Department had reconstructed Chicago's harbor pier and the Lighthouse Board was planning to build a new cylindrical metal tower at its end in place of the old 1869 wood-framed pierhead range beacon. The federal government and City of Chicago continued to improve the harbor, realizing that port operations attracted millions of tons of commerce. The Light List from the Bureau of Lighthouses in 1910 indicates there were 22 lights used for navigational purposes on Lake Michigan in close proximity to Chicago. At least six of these lights were exhibited from towers of varying design.

Chicago Harbor Light Station, ca. 1914. Photo from the National Archives

Chicago Harbor light's fog signal boiler room, ca. 1914. Photo from the National Archives

In 1917, construction was completed on the superstructure for a crib about 2,300 feet from the outer end of the new Municipal (Navy) Pier and Congress appropriated $88,000 on June 12 of that year to move the 1893 Chicago Harbor Lighthouse onto the structure where it remains today.

The light tower is about 27 1/2 feet in diameter at the base tapering to 18 1/4 feet at the top and is a little over 48 feet in height. Its rectangular concrete crib foundation is 44 feet by 65 feet and is 20 feet above mean lake level. The height of the focal plane of the lantern above the lake was listed at 82 feet in 1929.

It is flanked by a fog signal building and boathouse that are both one-story gable-roofed structures. There were four keepers at the station, and each had their own room for privacy and shared an oil burning stove for cooking in a communal kitchen. Drinking water was taken directly from the lake and the District Inspector in his site survey of 1929 listed the "healthfulness" of the station as good.

The 1894 fog bell was reported by Keeper T.F. Bailey to have been replaced by a 12-inch steam locomotive whistle powered by a four-horsepower engine. It was first put in commission on July 3, 1899. After the move to its crib location, the station received a Type-F diaphone fog signal in 1925 that could produce sound almost an hour faster than its locomotive whistle and had an effective range of 25 miles. It's sound characteristic was a 1 second blast; 2 seconds of silence; 1 second blast; 15 seconds of silence. This new piece of technology got mixed reviews from people as reported by John Herrick in the *Chicago Tribune*. Ships' navigators were impressed. *"That's the gol-darned best old horn on Lake Michigan,"* said one shipmaster. But the general public had a different view. *"That's the*

*damned-est outrageous nuisance and someone ought to hang for it."* The addition of a radio beacon in 1927 complemented the light and fog signal as a navigational aid. Initially, the effective radius of this beacon was 20 miles but it was upgraded in 1963 so that its radius extended 100 miles. This device was used by mariners to obtain better cross bearings on their

position in the harbor area.

The heart and soul of this light station was it's third-order Fresnel lens. Originally destined for Point Loma, CA, it was re-routed to Chicago for use in the World's Columbian Exposition and then installed in the new Chicago Harbor Light Station after that event ended. On October 4, 1929, the Lighthouse Service made a detailed report on this optic in its *Description of Chicago Harbor Light.* The 8-sided, polygonal-shaped lens was designed with glass "bulls'-eyes" that produced a light flashing characteristic of alternating red and white for 20 seconds before repeating or; 0.8 second red flash; 9.2 seconds eclipse; 0.8 second white flash; 9.2 second eclipse. The color was produced through the use of red glass panels attached to the outside of

Today, Chicago's harbor lighthouse is currently illuminated through the use of this DCB 2-24 rotating aero beacon which has a characteristic of a red flash every 5 seconds.
Photo courtesy of Brent Finch

Stairs leading to the lantern room in the 1893 lighthouse.
Photo by Rick Polad, 2002

Interior of Chicago Harbor Light's original 3rd order Fresnel Lens. By 1939, the kerosene oil lamp that was the source of light for the lighthouse beacon was replaced by a 300-watt light bulb. U.S. Coast Guard Photo by E. De Luga, 1939

the lens. The entire lens revolved to create the flashes and was turned through the use of a clockwork mechanism located in a center cast iron pedestal that supported the lens. This mechanism was powered by a 125-pound weight that had to be rewound every three hours and 20 minutes. Using a 300-watt lamp in 1939, the red flash had an intensity of 40,000 candlepower and the white flash was 140,000 candlepower. The beacon's intensity ultimately was given more illuminating power through the use of a 1000-watt light bulb, producing a signal that could reportedly be seen for 25 miles in good atmospheric conditions.

This lens was used to guide ships in and out of Chicago for some 70 years before being dismantled and replaced by a rotating aero-beacon. The old Fresnel lens finally made its way to California (the destination it was originally intended for) and is now part of the collections at the Point Loma Lighthouse Museum at Cabrillo National Monument near San Diego. Unfortunately, the lens was disassembled in transit to California and today many parts of this award-wining optic are missing. The lens remains in storage to this day, a sad ending to what was once one of the most important optics guiding mariners into the busiest port on the Great Lakes.

Throughout the 1900s, lights marking Chicago Harbor were modified according to need and in 1938 a new beacon was housed in a small square metal-framed tower on the southeast guidewall entering Chicago River.

Today, lighthouses have given way to new forms of technology that are more effective aids to maritime navigation. The 1893 Chicago Harbor Lighthouse, however, remains on the U.S. Coast Guard's shrinking list of lighthouses that are still active. As such, it has seen service for well over a century and continues to serve both pleasure and commercial craft that enter Chicago's port.

Chicago Harbor lighthouse, 2001. Photo by D.J. Terras

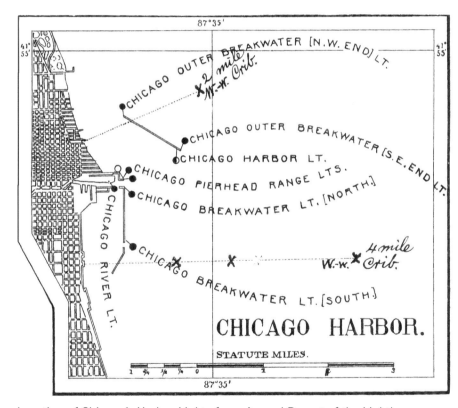

Location of Chicago's Harbor Lights from Annual Report of the Lighthouse Board, 1893. Note the addition of the two and four mile waterworks cribs. Map from the National Archives

## Chicago's 1893 Lighthouse and the World's Columbian Exposition

One of the truly great World's Fairs was the Columbian Exposition held in Chicago in 1893. The fair gave the purveyors of culture, art, science, technology and industry around the globe a chance to showcase all manner and class of object for public entertainment and education.

The Lighthouse Board was given space both inside and outside of the Government Building at the fairgrounds to mount their exhibits.

Thinking on a relatively grand scale, they requested a 100-foot by 50-foot space inside and a 150-foot square area on the outside.

*"On the inside are to be placed all lenses, lamps, chimneys, tools, wicks, lanterns, etc. On the outside will be a tower, to be afterwards placed at Waackaack station, in New York Bay, buoys of various kinds, whistles, sirens, etc."*
– A. Burgess, 1893 Report to the Lighthouse Board

The Board requested $15,000 from the federal government to fund this exhibit. It was found, however, that neither the space nor the funds were available for such an expanded public display, and the Lighthouse Board had to settle for a 51-foot by 24-foot area for the interior exhibit and a 150-foot by 50-foot space for the exterior display. Furthermore, by the end of the Columbian Exposition in October of 1893, the federal government had allowed the expenditure of just $5,686.95 by the Lighthouse Board. Arnold Burgess (1893) writes

*"So, it was finally agreed that the light-house exhibit, instead of being historic and exhaustive, instead of showing the growth of the service from stage to stage, instead of showing the process of its evolution, should show by the exhibition the point of growth to which it had arrived."*

In other words, the lighthouse exhibit would be created to emphasize its present organization, giving only cursory treatment to its past history.

Mr. Jacob Jose, an assistant civil engineer in the Lighthouse Service who had been in charge of other lighthouse exhibits, was put in charge of organizing and constructing the lighthouse exhibits at the Columbian Exposition. He was ordered to Chicago on April 24, 1893 and he

Light tower (far right) at the 1893 Columbian Exposition. Photo from the Special Collections and Preservation Division, Chicago Public Library

Photo of H. Lepaut's award-winning third–order Fresnel Lens (right rear) from Paris Exhibition of 1889. Photo from the Bibliotheque Nationale de France

stayed there through the duration of the exhibit and into December.

It was against this backdrop that the Lighthouse Board decided to have a working lighthouse erected and on display for public viewing during the event. A 100-foot steel skeletal light tower was built and stood guard at the entrance to a small harbor on Lake Michigan's shore that was created exclusively for the exposition. The Lighthouse Service had five keepers on site to operate the light as if it were an active aid to maritime navigation. There is a notation in the Lighthouse Index Files dated June 21, 1893, that second Assistant Keeper Samuelson had been given leave from his Chicago Harbor Lighthouse duties to be part of the detail that attended the Columbian Exposition Light. *"One of the keepers of the Chicago Harbor light-house was on duty in full uniform in connection with the light-house exhibit in the government building. He will be pleasantly remembered by many visitors for his courtesy, and especially for the intelligent answers he gave to their many questions. This man was a good specimen of his class."*

One of the showpieces of the Lighthouse Service display was a third-order Fresnel lens manufactured by the firm of Henri LePaute in Paris, France, in 1889. This lens had previously won awards at an exhibition there and, perhaps hoping to duplicate the Paris success, government officials here interrupted the lens' original routing to Point Loma, CA, for use in Chicago. However, despite these previous awards and being featured in the September 24, 1893 *Chicago Tribune* as "One of the Seven Wonders of the Fair," the lens did not duplicate its previous success. Awards, instead, went to the Lighthouse Service for the development of new buoys.

When the Columbian Exposition closed, this lens was moved to the new Chicago Harbor Lighthouse.

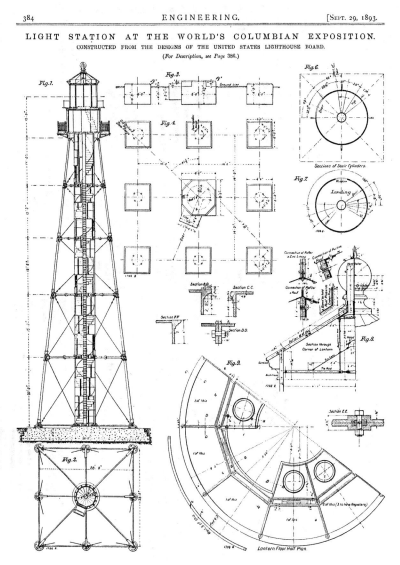

Illustration of Chicago's Columbian Exposition Lighthouse from *Engineering,* September 29, 1893.

Photo from the Special Collections and Preservation Division, Chicago Public Library.

Interior photo of Lighthouse Service exhibit at 1893 Columbian Exposition in Chicago. Annual Report of the Lighthouse Board, 1893. Photo from the National Archives

# Chicago's Crib, Pierhead and Breakwater Lights

Illustration of Chicago's two-mile water intake crib, ca. 1866. Plans for this facility were developed in 1855 by City Engineer, E.S. Chesbrough, but it took 12 years before the crib began providing Chicago with fresh water. Special Collections and Preservation Division, Chicago Public Library

So far we have discussed Chicago's major historical maritime aids to navigation operated by the U.S. Lighthouse Service. There were, however, other important lights helping the mariner to maneuver in and around Chicago Harbor that were maintained by the city. These were located on different types of structures including Chicago's water intake cribs, piers, and breakwaters.

For many people, the most interesting lights were those marking water intake cribs. These cribs, so-called because of the type of construction used to build them, constituted important maritime development projects and their location miles from the harbor entrance and close to port shipping lanes meant that they needed to be distinguished by navigational aids.

The stage was set for construction of these cribs by an Act of Congress approved January 16, 1864, permitting Chicago to "*extend aqueducts or inlet pipes into Lake Michigan so far as may be deemed necessary to insure a supply of pure water, and to erect a pier or piers in the navigable waters of said lake, for the making, preserving and working of said pipes or aqueducts: Provided, that such piers shall be furnished with a beacon light, which shall be lighted at all such seasons and hours as the light on the pier at the entrance to the Chicago River.*"

The earliest of these cribs was constructed two miles off shore, just north of the entrance to Chicago's harbor. The Sixth Annual Report of Chicago's Board of Public Works states that the water tunnel running two miles from shore was completed on November 30, 1866, the total cost being $457,844.95. Its use as an aqueduct furnishing the city with Lake Michigan water began on March 25, 1867. During construction the crib's foundation was being built on the north side of the Chicago River shoreline, about 800 feet west of the lighthouse. The structure was 58 feet in horizontal measurement on each of its five sides, and 40 feet high. The inner portion, or waterwell, had sides parallel with the outer ones and were each 22 feet long, leaving the distance between the inner and outer faces of the crib (or thickness of the protective breakwater) 25 feet. This breakwater was built on a flooring of 12-inch white pine timber laid close together. The outer and inner vertical faces and the middle wall between them were all of solid 12-inch white pine timber, except the upper 10 feet of the outside which was of white oak, a more suitable material to withstand the destructive action of ice. The entire structure was caulked, bolted together, launched into the water and settled into position with the aqueduct two miles from shore in 21 feet of water on July 24, 1865. When complete, the crib had a keeper's residence topped by a small wooden light tower and lantern with optic to mark its location

This depiction of a Chicago waterworks crib light tower has many times mistakenly been identified as the original 1866 crib structure. In fact, it has been described in both the 1892 and 1904 editions of the Annual Report of Chicago's Public Works Department as the Lakeview Crib, constructed in 1892.

for mariners in waters close to Chicago Harbor. However, many of the details of this structure were designed to be temporary and Public Works, instead of including an illustration of the actual design of the structure, published an idealized illustration. As a result, there are only several somewhat fanciful depictions of how this structure looked as originally built.

Public Works in its 1871 report stated that "*It was the design to remove as soon as possible the temporary lighthouse and all the wood-work above the surface of the water, and to construct in place thereof a substantial and permanent structure of stone, brick, and iron.*" But nothing immediate was done to upgrade the facility because it seemed secure. After seven years, how-

ever, the exposed portions above the water line were noticeably decaying and "*as a matter of safety the permanent structure, as originally designed, should be commenced at once.*"

Much of this work was accomplished before The Great Fire in October of 1871. However, the wooden structures above water remained exposed during this catastrophe and were at risk of being set ablaze by windborne live coals carried from the burning city. Fortunately, a vigilant keeper watched during the night and extinguished the flaming embers as they landed on the crib. By 1873, it was reported that the tower for the "reception" of the light had been constructed, awaiting the lantern and optic from the federal government.

Chicago Department of Public Works 1866 water works crib after improvements–including light tower. At right is an architectural line drawing of the 2-mile water intake crib.
Photo and architectural illustration from the National Archives

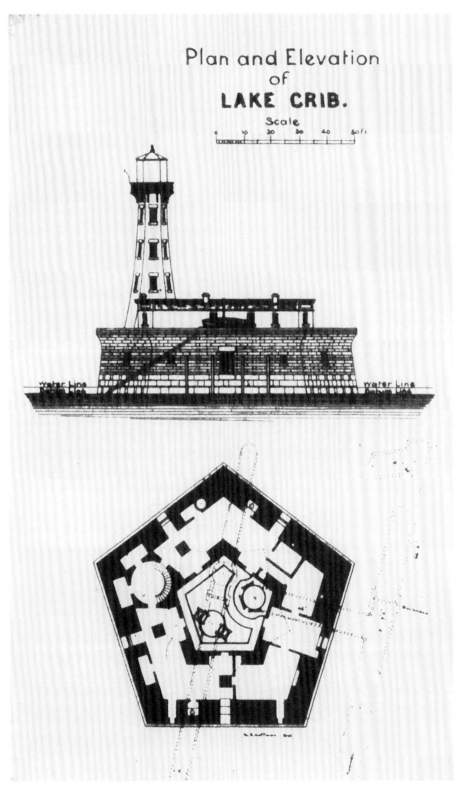

Plan and Elevation of LAKE CRIB.

Scale

At this time, the structure was distinguishable by a five-sided stone exterior above the waterline. The lowest three courses of outside masonry on the crib itself are of granite. Limestone was selected for the remaining external portion of the crib and for the lowest part of the interior walls. The arches and upper interior walls are of brick. The filling between the interior walls and the spandrel backing of the arches is of rubble. All of the masonry was laid in hydraulic cement. The deck of the crib is composed of a layer of ordinary concrete, on top of which was placed a layer of asphalt concrete. The crib was under the watchful eye of a keeper who lived in quarters that included an adjoining boathouse that was built for his convenience. Completion of this structure took longer than was anticipated, however. From the beginning, the City of Chicago and federal government had disagreements over who should be responsible for maintaining a navigational aid on such a city-built structure. The city, for its part, went ahead with architectural improvements to the crib, apparently assuming the federal government would pay for some of the cost, particularly the lantern and light optic. But the federal government put off paying for them. The December 31, 1876, Public Works Report states that *"The lantern is not yet finished, owing to the long-deferred hope of obtaining from the National government a light of the third order, the tower having been planned and thus*

Illustration of Chicago's two-mile water intake crib (view east) with light tower. Special Collections and Preservation Division, Chicago Public Library

Illustration of 1867 crib from the *Chicago Inter-Ocean*, November 9, 1890

*clear of anchor ice, for which one assistant is necessary, and sometimes more."*

However, by 1877 a more serious note is injected into the Public Works Annual Report. *"Soon after the completion of the present stone super-structure on the original* [1866] *wooden foundations, cracks in the outer walls and a settling of the floor near the* [keeper's] *living room appeared."* As a result, about three-fifths of the loose filling between the outer and inner walls of the crib was taken out, as well as the rubble backing of the outer walls and more solid work substituted. A little more than ten years after it had been built, the crib was clearly beginning to have structural problems. And the city engineer went on record in the 1880 Public Works Report stating that the *"crib was not a substantial and durable structure when erected, and, unless it be protected by massive sea walls of stone, it is liable, in my opinion, to be swept away in the near future during one of our severe winter storms."*

By 1880, a cupola [lantern] was being constructed for the brick tower of the crib lighthouse. Finally, the Journal of the Lighthouse Board for 1882 states that *"proper steps be taken to obtain authority to establish a light on Chicago Water Works Crib."* It was also reported that the Lighthouse Board had reached agreement with Chicago to furnish the facility with a third-order Fresnel lens and accessories once the city finished modifications to the tower and construction of the lantern. In addition to city plans, federal government plans for the crib were carried

through and the structure finally got its lantern and optic.

By 1888, however, the Public Works Report stated that the light tower shakes and sways very badly in a high wind and recommends removal of the masonry tower in favor of a light iron skeletal designed tower with an electrically powered light. The city, earlier during 1888, had constructed such a light 60 feet above the lake on a water inlet pier and they were impressed. *"Its rays are so brilliant that it is the first light seen from vessels approaching from the northward."* In fact, the original two-mile crib was relatively short lived, and by 1896 the structure had been demolished to a depth of 18 feet below the water surface where the remains were marked with a buoy. The demise of this structure was preceded by construction of a new waterworks crib

*far built with this view, under advice of United States officials."* A small beacon shining forth from the tower exhibited a fixed white light and there was even a fog bell, both maintained by a keeper employed by the City of Chicago.

The 1876 report goes on to describe his duties as keeping a light lit on top of the tower during the

season of navigation, in making and recording daily observations on the height and temperature of the lake water, on the height of the barometer, temperature of the air and force and direction of the wind. *"In the winter season he has no light to keep up, but has often the more arduous duty of keeping the inlets to the* [water] *tunnel shaft*

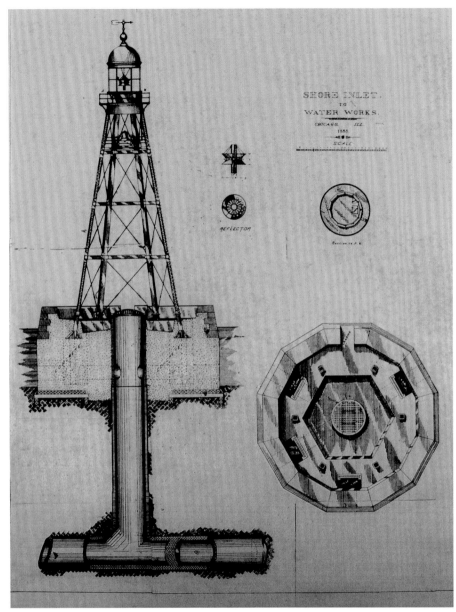

Diagram of 1888 shore water inlet lighthouse. Illustration from Archives of Department of Public Works, City of Chicago, 1888

about four miles from shore and this time, with full cooperation of the federal government, a light station was to be a part of the design.

With politics aside, Chicago eventually came to have warning beacons of different types at other water intake cribs along its shore, some of which still operate today.

Chicago's four-mile water crib was completed in 1894. U.S. Coast Guard photo

### Pierhead Lights

Pierhead lights were placed at the forefront of ships entering port and in the immediate vicinity of other structures important to port activities and maritime commerce. And they played an extremely valuable role in safely directing ship traffic in and out of areas where there was a high concentration of waterborne craft. Because of their location at the end of piers, they were always at high risk for collision with ships.

*"At Chicago, a new beacon was erected at the south end of the breakwater, to replace the old one carried away by a vessel last fall".* –Report of the Lighthouse Board, 1879

The pierhead light played a particularly important role in the history of maritime Chicago. In the early stages of port development sandbars were a constant problem when trying to enter Chicago's harbor and the only way to access the port was to use a channel that had been dug through the obstruction. Eventually piers were

Chicago's south pierhead lighthouse on breakwater, ca. 1930. U.S. Coast Guard photo

246.

Post card view of south pierhead light, ca. 1895. From the Nancy Osika Post Card Collection.

constructed that extended out into the lake to keep the channel free of sand. From 1832 to the early 1900s Chicago's harbor entrance to Lake Michigan saw continual lengthening of piers, and lights were needed on these structures as a way to direct mariners into the river channel and to warn them of shallow water. In Chicago, pierhead lights were designed in a variety of shapes and sizes according to their level of importance to mariners. The 1859 Chicago River pierhead light was a major aid to maritime navigation and the lead light

into Chicago's harbor. But this light was replaced in 1893 by a lighthouse that was built at the end of a breakwater at the harbor's entrance.

As a general rule, most pierhead lighthouses do not have keepers' quarters and the optics they contain are not as large or powerful as lake shore or sea coast lights. Some lights on piers were simply lanterns suspended on poles. These so-called pole becons, or post lamps and later types, developed according to need. One such design was used at Chicago on the end of North Pier and was

established on November 6, 1869. Its construction was simple, consisting of a wood-framed structure on stilts to obtain the desired elevation. A lantern room with optic and keepers' workroom, or a watch room, was the only interior space provided and a ladder gave access from ground level. This type of design provided an effective and economical structure that could be used by the Lighthouse Service for many years. In fact, a lighthouse of similar design made of metal was constructed in 1938 on the southeast guide wall into the Chicago River where it still operates to this day in a modified form

Because of shifting sands within Chicago's harbor, a pierhead range system was used to help insure that a vessel was steering a correct course to avoid becoming stranded in shallow water. A range system is based on the use of two lights, one set higher and in front of the other. They would be spaced apart the distance needed for a mariner to steer a safe course through a shipping channel. As long as the lights were seen one atop the other the mariner was safely located within the channel of deep water. If the lights were to the left or right of one another, navigational adjustments might have to be made. This pierhead range system was first officially reported for use at Chicago's harbor by the Lighthouse Establishment on March 3, 1871, when an appropriation of $35,000 was made to move the main Chicago Harbor Light from Chicago's pier to Grosse Point (some 12 miles north) and for changing the current arrangement of Chicago's River Light and the wooden pierhead light into a "beacon-range" system. This arrangement lasted until 1893 and the construction of Chicago's new main harbor light, situated at the end of a breakwater at the mouth to the Chicago River. The river light was then dismantled but the wooden pierhead beacon remained and received a fifth-order Fresnel lens in 1902. Four short years later, in 1906, the Lighthouse Board reported that *"owing to the dilapidated condition of the old wooden beacon, plans and estimates for a cylindrical metal* [light] *tower were made and material therefore was purchased. A pierhead range tower was also purchased."* According to the Lighthouse Service Light List for 1910, the metal rear range light tower was a white cylindrical structure that rose 41 feet above its base and exhibited a fixed white light that was visible for 12 miles in good atmospheric conditions. The front-range light was located 36 yards, 271 degrees, 100 feet east of the rear range tower. It was a slim, cylindrical structure also made of cast iron and stood 28 feet tall. It exhibited a fixed red light with a one-directional beam, visible for eight miles, that would be brightest when viewed head on. Together these two lights helped vessels navigate in and out of the confines of Chicago's River Harbor for over 25 years before harbor improvements were made so that the front-range was no longer needed. During the 1950s, the rear range

metal light tower was deactivated and taken down.

## Breakwater Beacons

The placement and construction of breakwaters surrounding the entrance to Chicago's River Harbor was ultimately responsible for providing an area of refuge from turbulent lake waters–an outer harbor to gather one's bearings before going up river or out into the open waters of Lake Michigan. Breakwater installations constitute formidable barriers to the natural elements and although built to help the mariner, could also be a hazard to ships if not properly charted and identified. And as Chicago's River Harbor grew, so did the breakwaters in Lake Michigan that protected her port.

Lights placed to mark Chicago's breakwaters varied in design and were both major navigational aids, such as the 1893 Chicago Harbor Light, or minor lights consisting in the past of nothing more than a post lamp.

## Chicago Breakwater, 1877

*"Two small lights are placed to mark the ends of the breakwater at this place; that on the southerly end being shown from an open frame-work structure, and the one at the northerly end from a post eighteen feet high. All necessary preparations were completed last fall, and the lights were exhibited upon the opening of navigation this year."*

– Annual Report of the Lighthouse Board to Congress, 1877

Chicago's Pierhead Range Lights, September 14, 1914. Like all range lights, the pair pictured above are set one in front of the other. When both lights are viewed from the proper perspective, they provide the correct course heading.
U.S. Coast Guard photo

Chicago outer breakwater (Northwest end) light, ca. 1933.
U.S. Coast Guard photo

STEAMER "CITY OF CHICAGO" CHICAGO-ST. JOE LINE

Chicago Harbor south breakwater light. Photo by D. Terras, Architectural cross-section from the National Archives

Steamer *City of Chicago* with south breakwater light at right. From the Nancy Osika Post Card Collection.

## Chicago Outer Breakwater

*"The outer breakwater at its lake end should be provided with a second or third order light and steam fog-signal. These aids cannot be placed on the breakwater itself, but must have a separate foundation. An act has been passed authorizing the establishment of this aid to navigation, but no appropriation has been made for doing the work. The Board therefore renews its recommendation for this purpose."*

– Annual Report of the Lighthouse Board to Congress, 1888

## Chicago Outer Breakwater, Northwest End

*"The light was changed from fixed white to fixed red on December 8, 1900. A five-day 360-degree lens lantern was substituted for the 1-day 360-degree lens lantern."*

– Annual Report of the Lighthouse Board to Congress, 1888

*"This light was established on April 21, 1890, to take the place of signal lights maintained by United States engineers during the construction of the* breakwater. This was completed in December, 1889."

– Annual Report of the Lighthouse Board to Congress, 1890

*"The steel tower formerly used at Racine Reef with Pintsch gas apparatus was erected at this station on four concrete piers."*

– Annual Report of the Lighthouse Board to Congress, 1907

## Chicago Breakwater (North)

*"The post at this station was destroyed by the schooner Lake Forest on June 22, 1899. A new post, with braces, was provided, also material for a sea wall protection. The post was erected and the work was completed on July 10,1899. A bill for damages amounting to $30 was sent to the owners of the boat."*

– Annual Report of the Lighthouse Board to Congress, 1900

# Lighthouses of Chicago Harbor South: The Calumet River

Chicago's Calumet Harbor, 1874. The creation of the Calumet and Chicago Canal and Dock Company in 1869 set the stage for the adoption of Calumet Harbor as a second port serving Chicago. Illustration courtesy of the Chicago Historical Society

## BIRDSEYE VIEW OF SOUTH CHICAGO—(CALUMET HARBOR.)

1. South Chicago Hotel.
2. Site Sinclair's Woolen Mills.
3. Railroad Station Buildings of Pittsburgh & Fort Wayne and Michigan Southern Railroads.
4. Location of Docks, Rolling Mills, Blast Furnaces, Elevators, etc.
5. Location of Ship Yard Dock.
6. Location of Cotton Mills.
7. Location of proposed Ship Canal to Lake Calumet.
8. Casgrain House.
9. Office of Calumet and Chicago Canal and Dock Co.
10. South Chicago Planing Mill and Lumber Yard.
11. Lake Calumet—three miles long and navigable for vessels.
12. Logan Park.
13. United States Government Engineer's Office.
14. United States Light House.

Although not incorporated as a city until 1925, the history of Calumet goes back to the mid-1800s when small lakeshore communities were trying to cash in on the lucrative and expanding shipping business. The Calumet region lies only about 12 miles south of Chicago and had many of the same assets that made Chicago a desirable location for a harbor. But for some reason, Calumet was slow to develop. Everett Chamberlain in his book, *Chicago and its Suburbs* (1874), asks the following: *"Why did the government not choose the larger stream [Calumet River], with its attendant lakes and almost limitless dockage, for its first appropriations, and why was not Chicago started here?"* The question is a good one. In fact, the Calumet River flowing into Lake Michigan had a greater natural capacity to handle ship commerce than the Chicago River and did not experience the problem with sandbars to the same degree. Mr. Chamberlain goes on to state that Calumet was *"destined to become the central manufacturing mart of the entire west and northwest."* This somewhat prophetic statement began to come true during the 1880s when Calumet started to reap the benefits of being a viable port alternative to the Chicago River.

The first lighthouse to serve Calumet was erected largely as a result of efforts by Illinois Congressman (1843-1857) John Wentworth, who also went on to become Mayor of the City of Chicago in the years 1857-58 and 1860-61. Wentworth had real estate interests in the Calumet area and it may have been his idea to attract lake shipping business to the Calumet River not only for the benefit of the local residents but to increase the value of his land holdings. Whatever his reasons, he was successful and federal appropriations were made in 1851 to construct a lighthouse near the shore where the Calumet River flowed into Lake Michigan. A local mason by the name of Wilson constructed the lighthouse using stone quarried from nearby Blue Island that had been transported to the site by pole barges. The structure was completed in 1852 and by 1853 was fully operational. Its life span, however, was short. In this relatively early historical period a harbor was never fully developed at Calumet and the city could not compete with Chicago's port facilities. Furthermore, the Calumet and Chicago port entrances

Calumet's first lighthouse was constructed in 1852 at a cost of $4,500.00. However, the new light confused mariners trying to enter Chicago's river port and it was extinguished in 1855 and then re-lit again in 1873 before being replaced by a pierhead light in 1876. It is seen here ca. 1873. Photo from the National Archives

were so close that mariners had trouble identifying their respective lights and some ships became stranded on shoals trying to get into the Calumet River. Complaints were made and in 1855 the federal government decided to discontinue Calumet's light indefinitely. However, population in and around the Calumet region continued to grow. In response, Congress decided to appropriate $50,000 in 1870 for harbor improvements and to re-establish the lighthouse as a maritime navigational aid for the port. The river mouth was also deepened and two piers jutted out into the lake on either side, creating a harbor entrance that was 300 feet wide. In addition, on March 8, 1871, $10,000 of federal money was earmarked to rehabilitate the old lighthouse and erect a dwelling for the keeper. Delays

Calumet Pierhead Light, ca. 1915, showing elevated walkway from shore. From the Nancy Osika Post Card Collection.

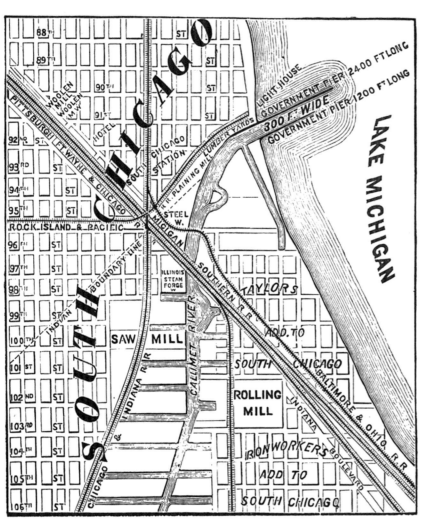

South Chicago and Calumet Harbor, ca. 1874.
Map from Chamberlain, 1874

in getting the work completed took the project into 1873 and the light shone forth from the shoreline for the next three years. In 1876, however, the Lighthouse Board decided that a better location for the beacon would be at the end of Calumet's north pier and the optic from the old lighthouse was transferred to a wooden pierhead lighthouse near the mouth of the Calumet River, leaving the light tower on shore without a beacon. The report of the Lighthouse Board for 1888 states that a landing dock at the inner end of the pier was built and the lighthouse was moved 300 feet nearer to its end. An elevated walkway was extended for access to it. Using the pier to access the lighthouse could be dangerous, so an elevated walkway was built for reasons of safety. In 1898, the wooden pierhead beacon was razed and a foundation for a new metal light tower was installed, consisting of 52 cubic yards of concrete with rubble stone embedded. Construction of this tower was completed and it began operating that same year. The cylindrical structure was constructed of cast iron casing with a concrete backing and rose 37 feet three inches from its base to a parapet with an inside diameter of 11 feet. The tower was painted buff (beige) for daymark color identification. Its sixth-order Fresnel lens exhibited a constant fixed red signal created through the use of a red glass chimney around the kerosene lamp that produced the beacon. A wood-framed fog signal building was constructed 20 feet west of the tower in 1899.

*"The fog signal building, 20 feet by 40 feet, was put up, fastened with strap anchors to the substructure, sheathed inside and outside, and the walls were*

CALUMET LIGHT STATION.
ILLINOIS.

Calumet River.

Calumet light station keepers' quarters and vicinity, ca. 1900.
Illustration from the U.S. Coast Guard
Photo courtesy of David and May Dietrich

characteristic of being struck once every 20 seconds. A clockwork mechanism operated the bell's striking arm, which needed to be rewound every two hours and 20 minutes for continuous functioning.

Over the years harbor improvements continued and Calumet's North Pier was extended, reaching over 3,600 feet into Lake Michigan. The south pier was also extended and reached a length of 2,020 feet. In addition to these improvements, a 7,000-foot breakwater was constructed early in the 1900s complete with a new lighthouse that became operational on July 20, 1906, marking the entry into harbor. At that time, Calumet's two lights became designated as South Chicago's Calumet Harbor (breakwater) Light and Pierhead Light. Both were instrumental in guiding ships through a channel that led into port facilities along the Calumet River.

A site survey performed by the Lighthouse Service on June 6, 1909, describes the 1906 Calumet Harbor Lighthouse as circular in shape and constructed of steel and cast iron. About 10 1/2 feet in diameter, it rose 40 feet and four inches in height from base to the ventilator ball of lantern. The fourth-order Fresnel lens inside of the lantern was produced by the L. Sutter Company in Paris and it emitted a fixed white light that was visible for 15 miles in good atmospheric conditions. In addition to the light, a fog signal building was constructed and the adjoining structures stood on the breakwater's

*filled in with sawdust and lime from the sill to the plate* [and] *a concrete and brick floor was laid. The boilers and machinery were installed and the signal was ready for operation on July 1, 1899."* – Annual Report of the Lighthouse Board, 1899.

These ten-inch steam-powered fog whistles were in operation 394 hours during 1904, consuming about 49 tons of coal and three cords of wood. Their use was to be short lived, however, and in 1907 they gave way to an 1,800-pound metal fog bell. This device, when in use, had a

This series of photographs was taken by N.M. Works on August 14, 1923 to document the alteration of the 1906 Calumet breakwater light. The original design of the light station left it close to lake level and in heavy seas the buildings took a beating from the waves. To help preserve the structure, it was lifted up from the breakwater and set on a new foundation of reinforced concrete that offered more protection against the elements and provided extra interior space for storage. U.S. Coast Guard photos

Despite increasing the height of the light station in 1923 and bolstering the foundation, the breakwater light eventually became damaged to the point where it had to be largely rebuilt in 1930. The new flat-topped structure with roof guard rails stands in stark contrast to the old hip-roofed design with dormer. The addition of riprap around the base of the structure provided more protection from the waves. However, despite these design changes, the station still suffered from exposure to the natural elements in sometimes extreme form. This was certainly the case on a cold December day in 1939 when the entire light station was encased in a thick coating of ice.
U.S. Coast Guard photos

concrete foundation seven feet above lake level. The fog signal consisted of a steam-powered locomotive whistle that eventually gave way to a siren sounded through a copper trumpet. The ear-piercing sound from this device was produced through the use of compressed air generated by a 16 horsepower oil engine. When in operation, this fog trumpet had a characteristic of sounding a three-second blast followed by 12 seconds of silence then another three-second blast followed by 42 seconds of silence.

Due to the close proximity of the harbor entrance to Indiana and the length and location of the new breakwater, the light established at its end was really in Indiana waters. This new breakwater light station came complete with a room for keepers to sleep in, but the preferred dwelling for those who tended Calumet's lights was located on shore in South Chicago, IL, near a United States Life Saving Station. The green brick-and-shingle two-story keepers' quarters was spacious enough to allow the principal keeper seven rooms and each assistant keeper four rooms for their privacy. There was also a small coal shed and brick oil house for storage of fuel. A red boathouse brightened up what was reportedly an otherwise dreary site. The quarters were nearly a mile from the lights and the most efficient way to access them was by boat or by using the elevated walkway from shore that stretched along north pier

Calumet Pierhead light, ca. 1949.
U.S. Coast Guard photo

Calumet Pierhead light, ca. 1910.
U.S. Coast Guard photo

Calumet's Pierhead Light of 1898 witnessed much of the growth in port operations. The steel-producing industry had moved their business from Chicago to Calumet during the 1880s and began to dominate the harbor landscape. By the middle of the twentieth century, operations had expanded east from the shoreline, displacing Lake Michigan waters and creating a landfill nearly to the end of the pier on which the light was constructed–over 3,600 feet. This pierhead light remained in service until 1976 when it was demolished after being hit by a ship trying to navigate into port.

The Calumet South Pierhead Light (above) was built in 1904. It was originally 44 feet in height and fitted with a fourth-order Fresnel lens. Automated in 1967, today this lighthouse can still be seen but its lantern has been removed. U.S. Coast Guard photo

Unlike Chicago Harbor Light, Calumet's light and keeper's quarters were located in the heart of a heavy industrial complex operated by the Carnegie-Illinois Steel Company, predecessor of U.S. Steel. Ore processing produced tremendous air and water pollution in the area, and the Ninth District Inspector in his 1909 site survey of the Calumet premises indicated the "healthfulness" there to be "not very good." In fact, the keepers at Calumet never really fared very well with regard to living conditions and the 1899 Annual Report to the Lighthouse Board went so far as to state that the keepers house was in deplorable condition, "unfit for human habitation" and requested that Congress appropriate $7,500.00 to build a new dwelling. A tight-fisted, budget-minded Congress put off dealing with the issue until June 28, 1902, when the money was granted for the requested purpose, although the structure was not completed until 1903.

Due to the rapid industrial growth in and around the South Chicago Calumet area during the 1880s and 1890s, its port facilities eventually became more heavily used than those on the Chicago River.

As a result, Calumet's breakwater light became one of the most important navigational aids on the Great Lakes.

Both the breakwater and pierhead lights were electrified and generally upgraded in 1923. There was a special interest that year in the Ninth

Lighthouse District (encompassing Lake Michigan) to electrify those lighthouses that were close to urban areas, for both Grosse Point and Chicago Harbor lights had been electrified as well. At the same time electrification took place, a 200-watt radio beacon was installed at Calumet's breakwater light location.

Unfortunately, with more advanced forms of technology available today, Calumet's two most historic lights have perished. The pierhead light was struck by a ship and removed by the U.S. Coast Guard in August of 1976. It was replaced for a short period of time by a simple pole light but even that navigational aid is gone due to increased landfill in the area. The demise of the 1906 breakwater light came about because the breakwater it was located on was extended to such a degree that only a small opening was left for craft to enter the harbor. The result was that the entrance to Calumet marked by this light was no longer needed and the Coast Guard had the buildings demolished in 1995, replacing the old lighthouse with a "sewer pipe" tower and rotating beacon with plastic optic. Today, in addition to this optic, Calumet Harbor has a light at the south end of its breakwater that was originally constructed in 1904. This steel skeletal structure has been modified and today does not have a lantern. The beacon is now produced through the use of a plastic, solar powered optic.

# Lighthouse Keepers

"Range lights, beacons, fog-bells, storm-signals, –there is no end to them, nor to the brave, steady souls who keep them alight and never falter in the long and lonely performance of duty. For the lakes are rich in capes, islands, and dangerous channels, beautiful as a dream by day–a dream of blue water and lustrous green isles wooded to their edges–but treacherous by night; and the light-keepers of the Great Lakes deserve a volume to themselves."

–Louise Morgan Sill,
*"Through Inland Seas"*
Harper's Monthly,
April, 1904.

"Christmas in a Lighthouse" Illustration from *Harper's Weekly*, December 30, 1876. D.J. Terras Collection

There is a great deal of interest today in the life and job of light keepers. Perhaps this is due to the fact that there are no longer any lighthouses that have keepers employed by the federal government with the exception of Boston Harbor Light, staffed purposely as a gesture to recognize the "craft" of light keeping. In fact, the public perception of the job and the reality of it were, and still are, often at odds. The job of light keeping was generally the same no matter where the lighthouse might be located. The life of a keeper, however, was greatly affected by geography and it is this aspect that leads one to romanticize about life in a lighthouse in wild and remote locations. Romantic visions aside, the reality can be much different.

*"Take any kid 18 years old and put him in a lighthouse and he'll be in an insane asylum in three weeks. It's a terrible life. They see the same faces all the time, do nothing but cook, wash, clean and climb those winding stairs".*

– Robert C. Ashton, Keeper of Chicago Harbor Light, *Chicago Daily News*, January 5, 1963

*"Lighthouse Schmitehouse. There seems to be a national infatuation with lighthouses. Everybody wants to hug one, be on one, be a part owner of one, volunteer on one, or be associated with one. My story is a little different ... I was stationed* [at one] *for two years, two months, three days, six hours and twenty-seven seconds, but who's counting?"*

– Greg Waller, MKC USCGR, *The Beacon*, Vol. 18, No.1, 1999

Lighthouse keeping was, to say the least, an occupation that took one out of the ordinary routine of daily life. In 1832, when the first lighthouse was built at Chicago, there were no formalities involved in getting a keeper's position and much depended upon whom you knew rather than what prior experience you might have had. Mark Beaubien was just such a keeper. He was the proprietor of the famous Sauganash Hotel during the early years of Chicago history and was a prominent businessman in the city. A gregarious and outgoing man, he would often entertain friends and the general public with his violin playing. He was very well liked. He was also keeper of the 1832 Chicago Lighthouse immediately before it was replaced in 1859. What mysterious circumstances brought him to this job are unknown but he apparently had no qualifications for holding the position and it is likely he became keeper because of favor.

In fact, keepers were politically appointed and a good word or deed for the right individual might mean success in obtaining a light keeping position. Because of this, the quality of people entering the ranks as light keepers varied greatly, with some individuals demonstrating the sense of responsibility truly needed to perform a good job and others who did the minimum required to hang onto the position. This state of affairs changed in 1852 with the introduction of the Lighthouse Board and their policy that an individual seeking the position of light keeper needed to be nominated by the local Collector of Customs. The board then reviewed the job applicant and would or would not endorse the candidate. By the 1890s, the formality was for an individual to be granted a period of time to show competence in the position and pass an examination given by the lighthouse district inspector. If a candidate passed both the work and written tests, the inspector notified the Lighthouse Board and the Secretary of the Treasury then gave the keeper a full appointment. At the time, these kinds of requirements were usually associated with higher paying jobs. Sadly, a keeper's salary remained low and continued to be a factor in the quality of individuals applying for the job. For example, the Lighthouse Board's General Correspondence Files includes a letter dated October 2, 1893, from Inspector Brice of the Ninth Lighthouse District concerning the pay scale at Chicago Harbor Light and stating his recommendation *that the* [principal] *keeper be given an* [annual] *salary of $750.00, first assistant $575.00, second assistant $525.00, third assistant 500.00, fourth assistant $450.00."* This pay scale for light keepers was high at the time.

In fact, the work of a light keeper was not mentally or physically difficult. However, the job was made much easier if one could read. During the middle to late 1800s this was a skill many people were lacking and in an effort to get a better educated keeper the Lighthouse Board created many manuals for reference, making the ability to read almost a prerequisite for the position. These publications dealt with proper government procedure and the details of how to operate machinery at light stations. Their titles, among many others, included *Directions to Guide Light-house Keepers and Others Belonging to the Lighthouse Establishment* and *Directions for the Management of Lenses, Lights and Beacons.*

It is also of note that, although the profession was dominated by men, women on occasion were appointed to the position of light keeper. For example, Mary M. Ryan was appointed keeper of the Calumet Lighthouse on August 10, 1873 upon the death of her husband who had held the position. She remained keeper for nearly eight years at Calumet under what would appear to have been—judging from some of her log entries—very difficult times.

April 7, 1874
> *"So dull in this place it is killing me. Wind blowing violently."*

May 2, 1874
> *"Nothing but gloom without and within.*

April 22, 1880
> *"I Think some changes will have to be made. This is not a fit place for anyone to live in."*

July 31, 1880
> *"This has been the most trying month of my keeping a lighthouse, the most important question, can anything worse come?"*

George Rose assistant keeper at Chicago Harbor Lighthouse from January 4, 1895 to May 24, 1906. Photo courtesy of Wind Point (WI) Light Station

Mary Ryan finally left her post as keeper of the Calumet Lighthouse on November 7, 1880.

Not surprisingly, the most important job of a keeper was to make sure the life-saving beacon of light was visible from sunset to sunrise. Unless there were orders to the contrary, instructions provided that regular four–hour watches were to be maintained. So as not to have the less desired watches fall entirely upon one person, the watches were to be alternated daily. As Roger C. Gilliver, assistant keeper at Chicago Harbor Lighthouse, stated to the Chicago Daily News, January 5, 1963. *"When you're sitting watch after midnight–that's when you get bugged."* The Lighthouse Service definitely did not want anyone getting "bugged" too often.

In an effort to cut down on last minute problems it was necessary for the lighting equipment to be in good condition and the keepers were instructed to have everything put in order for lighting in the evening by 10 o'clock a.m. daily. The head, or principal, keeper usually performed work associated with maintenance of the light. This consisted of cleaning and polishing the Fresnel lens and removing all dust from its framework. The lens would need to be washed every two months with spirits of wine and polished annually with rouge. The lamp inside the lens would be cleaned, filled with fuel and if needed alternated every 15 days. Old wicks would be trimmed or new wicks installed making the lamp ready for lighting at dusk.

The principal keeper would also be assigned the duty of maintaining a log book that contained general information pertaining to the operation of the lighthouse. This could include entries that ranged from mundane to important issues. The following represents a good cross section contained in the logbooks from Chicago.

February 3, 1896

*"I have to-day received from the Illinois Broom Co. 35 day brooms."*

September 9, 1897

*"The telephone has been put up at this station no. main 1068."*

January 18, 1913

*"Station visited by Superintendent about electrification."*

June 30, 1917

*"Steamer Christopher Columbus wrecked in Milwaukee. Many lives lost"*

July 28, 1919

*"Asst. saved man from drowning at north tower."*

July 30, 1920

*"Assistant left station at 7 pm. His son drown at station."*

February 1, 1921

*"A very dark day, the air full of smoke. Lights all on. Like night all day."*

June 27, 1923

*"Mr. Butler called in regard to electrification."*

July 2, 1923

*"Electricians at work."*

July 23, 1923

*"Electrical work complete in main station."*

Like the principal keeper, assistant keepers were required to perform a nightly watch of the light. During the day, they were usually responsible for work that consisted of such chores as cleaning the inside and outside of the plate glass of the lantern. In addition, they would have to polish all copper and brass and clean the walls, floors, and balconies of the lantern, stairways, landing, doors, windows, window recesses, and passages.

When routine work associated with the light was finished, keepers would be required to perform basic maintenance chores consisting of repairs to the equipment and structures. Any repair requiring special skills would be handled by contract as specifically requested by the keeper. Major maintenance projects were channeled through the Lighthouse Board, which would request a special appropriation of money from Congress. The Board's General Correspondence Files contain a letter from Chicago keeper Thomas Bailey who wrote to the district inspector on March 12, 1897, *"Sir, I have written the engineers office in regard to repairing the tower at the outer breakwater. It has been leaking some time and when it rains the third assistant cannot stay in his bedroom."* On February 28, 1898, he wrote *"Sir, I write to you in regard to some repairing that is necessary to be done at this station this spring. A new roof for the kitchen and new cellar doors and steps and new storm doors."*

Brothers Philip and George Sheridan (with family) reportedly both served as asst. keepers at Chicago Harbor Lighthouse during the 1890s.
Photos courtesy of Jack Sheridan

75

Perhaps the best description of a Chicago light keeper was presented to the public eye in 1890.

A commanding figure among sailors is Captain Charles McKee, superintendent of the crib and keeper of the beacon light established there. He "roughed it" as a common sailor and as commander for thirty-three years before anchoring in "snug harbor." The keepers home at the crib, though isolated and seemingly lonesome, is really a charming retreat, as will be readily attested by those who have invaded its privacy, besides which, it possesses some advantages not shared by other places of residence. If, for instance, the inmates should desire, during the evening, to perform some work of a mental nature, they are not disturbed by the barking of a neighbor's dog, or by gangs of half-grown boys at the corner grocery. They are spared the infliction, during these election days, of the boy who carries a very large mouth and a very small bundle of papers through the streets, yelling "extra, extra paper," till it would seem the top of his head must come off. Dust, smoke, chattering horses hoofs, peddlers, and locomotive whistles have no terrors for the quiet folks out at the crib.

The Captain and his daughter, Mrs. Estelle Hanson, spared no exertions in making their visitor acquainted with the delightful place. A sketch made in the sitting room is only one of many that might be obtained of the interesting nooks and corners taken up with books, flowers, hanging baskets and other evidences of refined tastes. The captain's nautical inclinations are to some extent indicated by the character of numerous pictures adorning the walls, while an alcove discloses a piano and other musical instruments. In wintry nights the twinkling stars may look down on a wild and sullen waste of waters about their home, while ice-laden waves shall beat unceasingly against its outer walls, but within the seclusion of these apartments Music's cheerful presence can dispel the angry roar and bid defiance to the bleak surroundings. When ice comes Mr. McKee remains constantly at the crib, for ice has been known to come up on deck in twenty minutes. Ten years ago this winter the services of two men were required to clear the place of this enemy. They had to stand on deck with pikes and poles and struggle manfully to keep it from burying them, but despite their exertions it reached to the height of the house and stood there all day.

– *The Chicago Inter-Ocean,*
November 9, 1890

Illustration of 1866 crib from the *Chicago Inter-Ocean*, November 9, 1890.

Illustration of Charles McKee, keeper of Chicago's crib lighthouse. From the *Chicago Inter-Ocean,* November 9, 1890.

Illustration of keeper McKee's living quarters at the crib. *Chicago Inter-Ocean*, November 9, 1890.

Keeper McKee's problems with ice on the water intake crib were common. In fact, ice on the lakes was a constant threat to effective management of navigational aids during the cold weather months, and it was a particular nuisance for keepers at harbors like Chicago's that tended to freeze over very quickly. The Lighthouse Board's General Correspondence Files are filled with references that pertain to this problem along the Illinois shoreline. On March 7, 1890, Andrew Davenport, keeper at South Chicago's Calumet Light, reported to the District Inspector that *"I hereby notify you that I discontinue lighting my lights from today. The harbor being entirely overloaded with shore ice and frozen solid."* Keeper Thomas F. Bailey at

Chicago's River Harbor Light likewise reported on January 27, 1894, that *"The ice was so thick in the river that I could not light up the south pier lights last night."* And, on January 15, 1897, *"Sir, the best light at the south pier went out at 7 p.m. last night, I have not been able to get there for three days on account of the ice in the river."* It should be kept in mind that, in addition to constantly maintaining the main harbor light, keepers at Chicago had charge to care for the various other federally operated pier lights and beacons in the port.

Fog is another natural element that occurs regularly on the Great Lakes and was a constant concern to light keepers who would activate fog signals to warn navigators of approaching landfall. On July 15 and 16, 1899, the Chicago Harbor Keeper's Log reported that the fog signal needed to be activated from 6:15 a.m. to 7:15 a.m.; 7:45 a.m. to 9:15 a.m.; 11:30 p.m. to 12:45 a.m. (July 16); and then again from 2:00 a.m. to 6:00 a.m. This erratic pattern is somewhat atypical and must surely have been a trial for the keepers who had to stoke the fires of the steam-operated machinery to sound the fog signal.

The anticipated use of the fog signals was such that on October 10, 1895, Chicago Harbor's keeper, Thomas Bailey, requested 30 tons of coal and two cords of wood for their operation over the upcoming winter months. On March 19, 1897, keeper Bailey sounded an alarm when he

informed the district superintendent that he had *"but three tons of coal and if the fog lasts we can only run about 723 hours...it would be best to send out a supply as soon as convenient."*

Fog and ice, however, were not the only problems that Chicago's keepers had to contend with. Operating a lighthouse in a large metropolitan area meant constant contact with the general public and some people were of a very unsavory character. O. Hansen, Keeper of Chicago's Harbor Light, reported the following on September 5, 1892:

*"I have to report the actions of one Fred Drews of the firm of Leyden and Drews architects and contractors who positively refused to leave the docks of the lighthouse reservation and when I threw off their lines one of the crew who had been drinking jumped on the dock and threatened to kill me if I repeated the action again. This man Drews knows he has no right to keep his scams tied up at the dock but says he is going to do it whenever he wishes."*

In this situation Nicoll Ludlow, Ninth District Inspector, referred the matter to the District Attorney. Keeper Thomas F. Bailey, however, faced a more chronic problem as he relates in the following letter dated April 23, 1900, to the district inspector:

*"Sir: I wish to make a complaint to you of the condition around north beacon. The people that frequent the north pier seem to take delight in making it as filthy as possible around the beacon and post light. The stench in the watch-*

Andrew Jackson Davenport as Principle Keeper seen here in his complete official keepers uniform and sporting a walking stick. Photo ca. 1883. Courtesy of David and May Dietrich.

room and lantern shanty is unbearable. It is impossible to keep it clean. They pay no attention to what we say to them. The only way to keep them from committing nuisances will be to put a fence across the pier. It will be a good plan to fence in all the lights on both piers."

Keeper Bailey's recommendation was followed and the areas in question were fenced and restricted from public access.

Living and working at a harbor light located in an exposed area near the end of a pier also had its hazards as related here by Keeper Hans L. Hanson on September 7, 1888:

"At mid-night last night when the schooner A.J. Dewey of Chicago was towing out of harbor and close out to the end of north pier her towing line [broke] and before the tug could come around and get hold of her again she run her jibboom through the south side of the north pier beacon completely destroying that side of the watchroom and broke the steps leading from the watch room to the lantern also a part of the north side of the beacon."

Collisions with the pier were not unusual and one close call occurred on October 25, 1895, when an iron-hulled freighter scraped the side of the pier causing sparks that ignited a fire on the lighthouse platform. Other types of hazards were reported to the district inspector and the following letter carries with it a certain tone of urgency:

"I have to report the city contractors by name of Dryden & Drew & Co. who

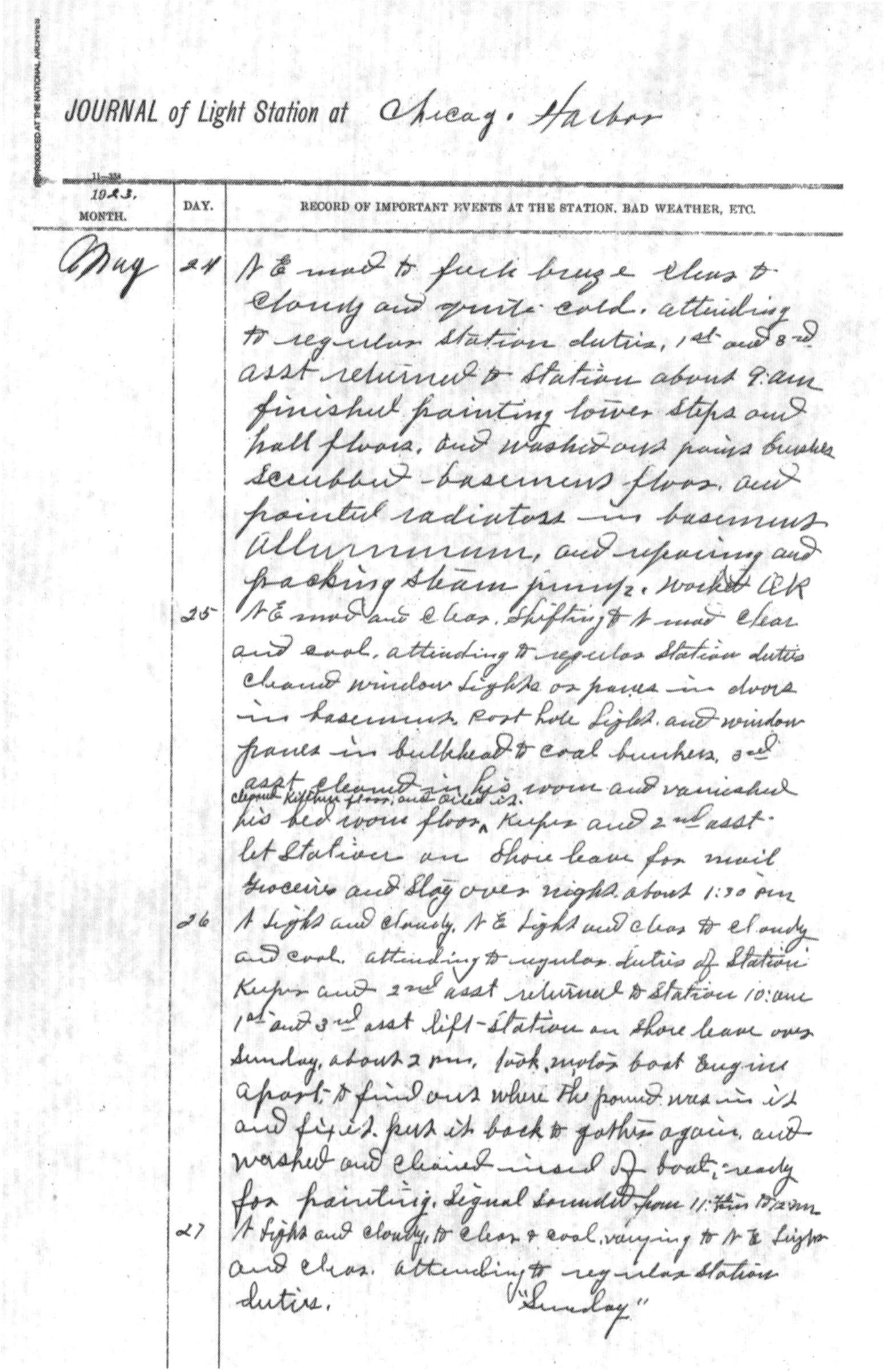

JOURNAL of Light Station at Chicago Harbor

One of the responsibilities of a light keeper was to make daily entries in a log. The page left and at right are from the Chicago Harbor Light Keeper's log, 1923. From the National Archives

## JOURNAL of Light Station at Chicago Harbor

| 1923. MONTH. | DAY. | RECORD OF IMPORTANT EVENTS AT THE STATION, BAD WEATHER, ETC. |
|---|---|---|
| May | 28 | N E light to mod. clear varying to N W mod. clear and cool. attending to regular duties of station. 3rd asst returned to station about 9 am. 1st asst returned to station about 11 am. Mixing paints, and painting S. Entrance Gas Light tower, and painting motor boat No 65. Keeper went ashore to stay over night about 4 pm. |
| | 29 | N E light and clear. shifting to N mod. and clear. shifting to S Light and variable winds clear to E cloudy. Keeper returned to Station 9 am. Finished painting S. Entrance gas Light tower, and finished painting, Staining and varnishing motor boat # 65. 2nd asst cleaned in his bed room, and painted base board. Washed out paint brushes. |
| | 30 | Light to mod N E winds clear & cool. attending to regular station duties. Keepers family & some friends visited at Station. "Decoration Day" |
| | 31 | Light N E to N winds clear and cool attending to regular duties of Station Painting N W end Gas Light tower 2nd asst returned to station 11 am. wiped down tower steps. washed out towels, and making out reports of station. Cleaned brass on No 1 tower. |

*are extending the water tunnel at Hyde Park one mile are making it very uncomfortable for my self and family ...by them handling and storing in large quantities of Aetna High Explosive cartridges and dynamite, at this writing there are three boxes of 50 pound each stored about one hundred feet from this dwelling in a shanty built by the city."*

–Andrew Davenport, Keeper, Calumet Lighthouse, October 20, 1898

These obstacles to proper operation of a light station–not to mention hazards to life and limb–were sometimes more a part of the keeper's job than one realized and they kept most people who held the position alert. In some circumstances, a well-organized keeper might be able to fulfill the requirements of his job and find time to pursue other interests. In fact, the Lighthouse Board did give tacit recognition that keepers might find time to pursue other employment providing that it would not keep them away from the lighthouse for a prolonged period of time. For the keepers of Chicago's Harbor lights, additional employment was not an option. The responsibilities they held in maintaining multiple lights to aid navigation was enough and it's a testament to these individuals that, given the heavy work load and low pay, they established an exemplary record with the Lighthouse Service.

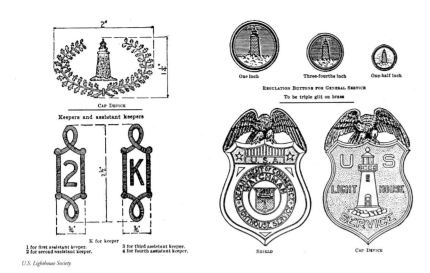

Lighthouse keepers uniform insignia.

**Thomas J. Bailey** of the Lighthouse Service, ca. 1906. Keeper Bailey served at the Chicago Harbor Light from 1893 – 1906 and although "Keeper" was the appropriate title for the position, Bailey–like his counterpart, E.J. Moore, at the Grosse Point Lighthouse some 12 miles north–preferred the title of "Captain." Indeed, Keeper Bailey did have a long and interesting career in the British Navy but never did rise to the rank of Captain. Born in Somersetshire, England, in 1849, he was fascinated with the idea of becoming a sailor and left home to serve in various capacities on ships for 20 years. During this time he weighed anchor in such locations as the Crimea, India, China, New Zealand, and Paraguay before retiring and coming to America in 1871. Once here, he entered government work with the U.S. Life-Saving Service at Ludington and White Lake (MI) before becoming Keeper of Big Point Sable Lighthouse (MI). In 1893, he was transferred to Chicago and given the position of Principle Keeper of the Chicago Harbor Lighthouse. For the next 13 years Thomas Bailey and his staff of five assistant keepers took charge of federally operated navigational aids that served the Port of Chicago. Photo courtesy of the Chicago Historical Society

### United States Lighthouse Service
### Principle Keepers of the Chicago Harbor Lighthouse

| | | |
|---|---|---|
| George Snow | August, 1833 – October, 1833 | Resigned |
| Samual Lasley | October, 1833 – October, 1834 | Resigned |
| William Stevens | January, 1835 – 1839 | Resigned |
| John Gibson | 1839 - 1841 | Resigned |
| William Stevens | September, 1841 – July, 1842 | Resigned |
| Silas Meacham | July, 1842 – December, 1844 | Resigned |
| James Long | December, 1844 – July, 1849 | Resigned |
| Charles Douglass | July, 1849 – May, 1853 | Resigned |
| Henry Fuller | May, 1853 – February, 1855 | Resigned |
| Mark Beaubien | February, 1855 – October, 1859 | Resigned |
| Morris Walsh | October, 1859 – March, 1861 | Resigned |
| John Lobstine | March, 1861 – November, 1866 | Resigned |
| Leonard Miller | November, 1866 – September, 1869 | Resigned |
| Charles Boynton | September, 1869 – January, 1874 | Transferred |
| Anthony Hagen | June, 1875 – December, 1887 | Transferred |
| Charles Lindstrom | December, 1887 – February, 1888 | Transferred |
| Hans Hansen | February, 1888 – July, 1890 | Transferred |
| Ole Hanson | July, 1890 – March, 1893 | Transferred |
| Thomas Bailey | November, 1893 – July, 1906 | Transferred |
| Alfred Erickson | August, 1906 – March, 1911 | Transferred |
| Edward Knudsen | March, 1911 – September, 1911 | Transferred |
| Orland Lynd | October, 1911 – March, 1913 | Transferred |
| Severin Danielsen | November, 1914 – September, 1919 | Records Incomplete |
| Thomas Armstrong | September, 1919 – 1928 | Records Incomplete |
| Robert McKillop | 1940 | |

**In 1939 the U.S. Coast Guard absorbed the U.S. Lighthouse Service and was given responsibility for managing all maritime aids to navigation.**

In light stations with more than one keeper, the principle keeper would be responsible for equipment exclusively employed to care for the Fresnel lens optical system and one of the most important items was the lamp that created the beacon of light for maritime navigation. The unidentified keeper here is shown with a three-wick kerosene lamp that would have required specific items for its maintenance and operation such as lanterns, chimney lifters, and containers for storing wicks and rouge. The U. S. Lighthouse Board's *Instructions and Directions for Light-House Keepers* (1858) states that the lamp had to be lit from sunset to sunrise and watched continually by the keeper during its operation–lighthouse keepers were called "wickies" because while on duty they had to be vigilant in trimming the wick(s) of the lamp to produce the brightest flame possible.

Other important items in the maintenance of the light and related equipment would be fuel containers and oil cans of various sizes and shapes. Assistant keepers would generally be responsible for the more routine maintenance concerns and use common everyday tools for cleaning and maintenance. All of these items however complicated or simple would be manufactured to specifications by the United States Lighthouse Establishment and were generally constructed of brass and carried the stamp from the Lighthouse Depot where they originated. For example, the oil can pictured immediately at left carries the stamp of the Staten Island, NY, Lighthouse Depot. The first such depot on the Great Lakes was established in 1874 in Detroit, Michigan.

Photo of keeper (unidentified) from Grosse Point Lighthouse collections. Photos below and at far right by D.J. Terras.

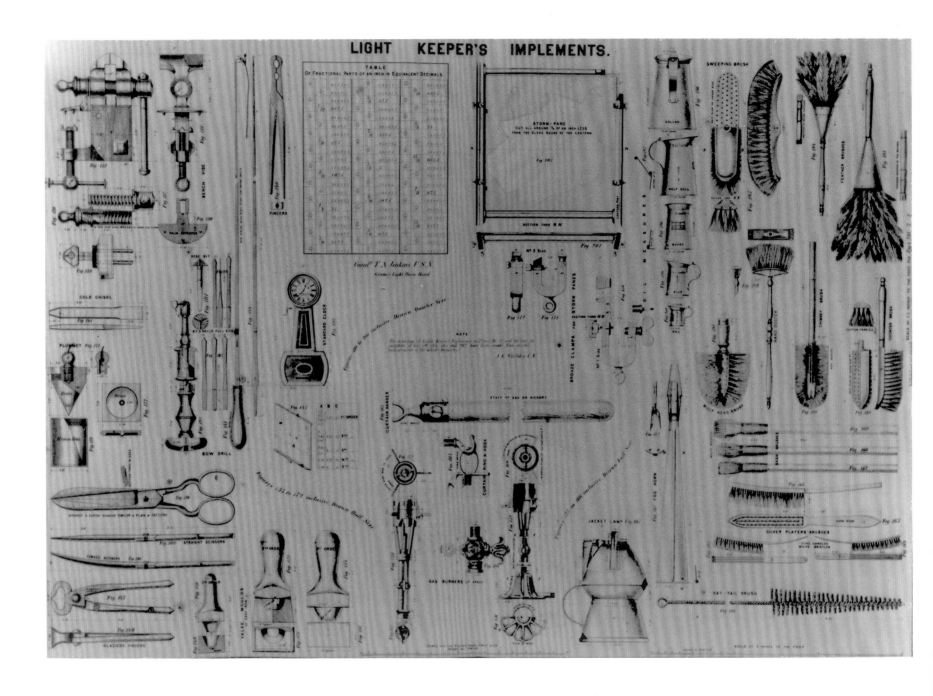

LIGHT KEEPER'S IMPLEMENTS.

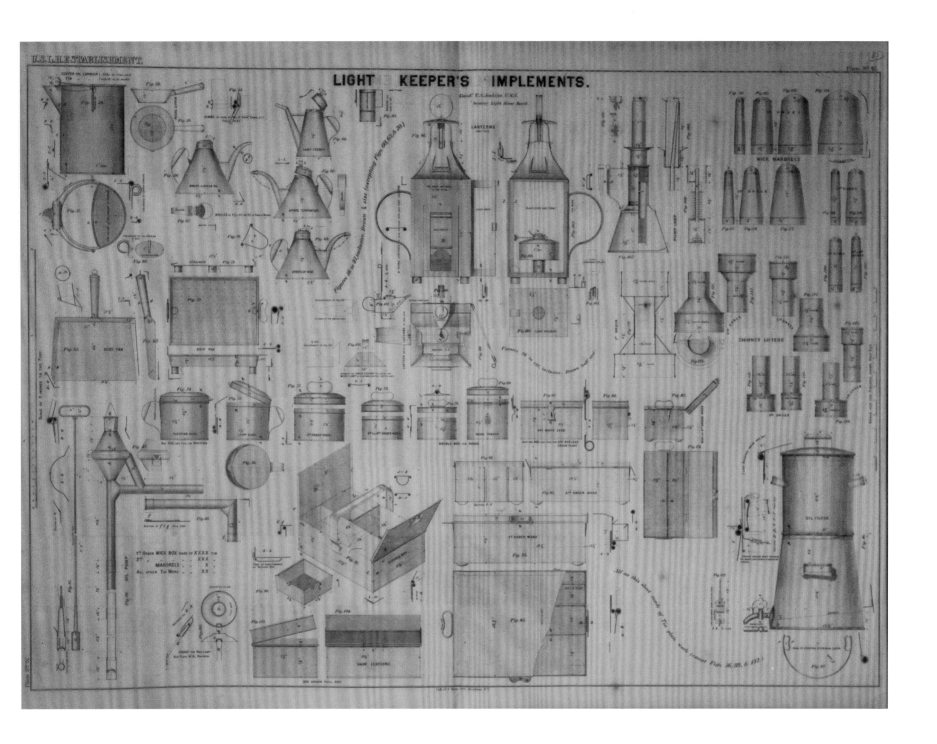

# LIGHT KEEPER'S IMPLEMENTS.

**Andrew J. Davenport** was principle keeper of the Calumet Pierhead Lighthouse (South Chicago) from October 2, 1888 to February 28, 1911. Born on the island of Mackinaw, MI, on December 6, 1854, Andrew received his first government position as asst. keeper of the Waugochance lighthouse in the Straits of Mackinaw on October 3, 1874, but his management ability and responsibility were recognized by the Lighthouse Service and by 1883 he was promoted to Keeper and re-assigned to the Two Rivers (WI) Light Station. He stayed at Two Rivers for five years before being transferred to Calumet, a station he would manage for over two decades. At Calumet he and his wife, Clara Hamann, raised four children: Albert, George, Elsie, and Edith. He died in May of 1929 but the strength and temperament of the man is revealed in a letter dated October 2 written by his granddaughter, Edith.

*"I had great respect for my grandfather because he was like his father, a very strong character and absolutely fearless. However, he was deaf in one ear and no hearing aid could help him because his eardrum had been removed by a quack doctor. He was a sort of loner by necessity. One night Grandpa was out at the light house blowing the fog horn when his sweater got caught in the machinery and pulled his hand in far enough to mash his thumb and he stayed there all night running the fog horn until morning. When he came in his thumb was a gory mess. Mother went with him to the doctor and he sat there and let them take the nail off with only an occasional grunt of pain—without any anesthetic.... During the war [WW I] the beach was just swarming with sailors and there was a poor dimwitted girl who hung around the beach all the time. One night when he [grandpa] was going to the lighthouse he found a sailor with the girl and he picked him up off her and threw him in the water."*

In addition to the traditional insignia worn by a light keeper of 25 years service, Keeper Davenport proudly sports an "Inspector's Efficiency Star" awarded to keepers acknowledged by the Bureau of Lighthouses to be highly proficient in executing their duties. Such keepers could wear the star for a year. Other honors during this time included the "Commissioner's Efficiency Star" and the "Efficiency Pennant" which was presented annually to the best run light station in each district.

Photo courtesy of David and May Dietrich

**United States Lighthouse Service**
**Principle Keepers of Calumet (South Chicago) Lights**

| | | |
|---|---|---|
| Dalton, A. | Calumet River Light | 1852 – 1853 Resigned |
| Squires, Hiram | Calumet River Light | 1853 – 1855 Light discontinued |
| | Calumet River Light | 1873 – 1876 Reactivated for three years |
| Ryan, Mary | Calumet Pierhead Harbor Light | 1873 – 1880 Removed |
| Rushmore, C. | Calumet Pierhead Harbor Light | 1880 – 1885 Removed |
| Moore, Edwin | Calumet Pierhead Harbor Light | 1885 – 1888 Transferred |
| Davenport, Andrew | Calumet Pierhead Harbor Light | 1888 – 1911 Transferred |
| Erickson, Alfred | Calumet Pierhead Harbor Light | 1911 – 1913 Transferred |
| Graan, Carl | Calumet Pierhead Harbor Light | 1913 – 1930* Transferred |
| Danielson, Severin | Calumet Harbor Breakwater Light | 1911 – 1914 Transferred |
| Robinson, Jerome | Calumet Harbor Breakwater Light | 1914 – 1928* Transferred |
| Pierce, Ardell | Calumet Harbor Breakwater Light | 1939 |

**Responsibility for Calumet"s lights was turned over to the U.S. Coast Guard in 1939.**

*Records Incomplete

## A First Family of Great Lakes Lighthouse Keepers

When Ambrose Davenport Jr. gave up fur trading and fishing to become a lighthouse keeper at the Skillagalee Light Station (MI) in the early 1800s, little did he realize that he would be passing on this new occupation to his descendants. Born on Mackinaw Island (MI) November 28, 1801, he would marry Susan O-gee-em-a-qua des Carreaux, the daughter of a French father and Chippewa mother, and produce a family of light keepers.

### John Davenport, B. 1840
Asst. Keeper at Skillagalee (MI) Light – 1860
1st Asst. Keeper at "Washin" (MI) Lighthouse – 1861
Acting Keeper of Pentwater (MI) Lighthouse – 1873

### James Davenport, B. 1848 (1838?)
Asst. Keeper, Waugochance (MI) Lighthouse – 1871
Keeper, Little Sable (MI) Lighthouse – 1873
Keeper, McGulpin Point (MI) Lighthouse – 1879
Keeper, Mission Point (MI) Lighthouse – 1907

### Julia Davenport, B. 1845
While it was not uncommon for women to become light keepers, Julia kept the profession in the family by marrying Light Keeper, William Henry Duncan, Asst. Keeper of the Waugochance Lighthouse and later Keeper (1877 – 1881) of the Beaver Island (MI) Lighthouse. William and Julia eventually came to live at Eagle Bluff Lighthouse in Wisconsin where they and their 7 sons were keepers for 35 years.

### Andrew J. Davenport, B. 1854
Asst. Keeper, Waugochance (MI) Lighthouse - 1878 (1874?)
Keeper, Two Rivers (WI) Lighthouse – 1883
Keeper, Calumet South Chicago (IL) Pierhead Lighthouse – 1888 – 1911

### Albert Davenport, B. September 18, 1875
Son of Andrew Davenport, Albert established himself as a third generation Davenport light keeper while serving at Calumet Pierhead Lighthouse, 1902; North Manitou Lighthouse, 1916; and Grosse Point Lighthouse, 1920.

Keeper Andrew J. Davenport seen here with his family. From left: George C., Andrew J. Elsie, wife Clara holding Edith, and oldest son Albert. Photo courtesy of David and May Dietrich

A changing of the guard took place in 1939 when the U.S. Lighthouse Bureau was merged with the U.S. Coast Guard. This marked the end of a special branch of the government whose sole responsibility was to oversee management of lighthouses. Pictured here we see the last Bureau keepers of Chicago Harbor Lighthouse. From Left: T.J. Bremman, skilled laborer; Clarence Mason, 3rd assistant keeper; Jack Short, 2nd assistant keeper; James Brotherson, 1st assistant keeper; Robert McKillop, Principal Keeper. Photo from the U.S. Coast Guard

Keeper James Brotherson, keeps an eye on fog signal machinery at Chicago Harbor Light in 1939. Photo from the U.S. Coast Guard

Keepers in 1963 use a makeshift kitchen in what was originally Chicago Harbor Light's boathouse. Coast Guard keepers at Chicago had a cooking compensation subsistence wage of $77.10 a month, so "the men can at least eat steak when on the job." *Chicago Daily News*, 1963

On August 7, 1789, U.S. President George Washington and the First Continental Congress enacted legislation that made the federal government responsible for building, operating and maintaining aids to navigation in the United States. Within a year, the original 13 colonies had turned over a dozen operating lighthouses. It is upon this collection of lighthouses that the United States built a system of aids to maritime navigation that eventually ranked with the best in the world. This did not happen overnight, however. Management for aids to navigation fell first to Alexander Hamilton and the Treasury Department under the Commissioner of Revenue and the Secretary of the Treasury. But in 1820, responsibility for lighthouses and other aids to maritime navigation wound up in the hands of a man named Stephen Pleasonton, fifth auditor of the treasury. Pleasonton's 32-year tenure ushered in a period of poor management and blatant conflicts of interest. Ships' captains and owners complained bitterly about the inadequacy of the nation's lighthouses and Congress finally acted on the matter in 1852 with the establishment of a Lighthouse Board. The Board was composed of military personnel and civilian scientists both working together for the best interest in safeguarding passengers and commerce traveling over this country's waterborne transportation routes. The Lighthouse Board increased the number of aids to navigation and also made sure they were technologically up to date. Eventually, the expanded use of navigational aids became too much of a bureaucratic burden and a new administrative branch, called the Bureau of Lighthouses, succeeded the Lighthouse Board in 1910. The Bureau, which came to be officially known as the Lighthouse Service, was subsequently merged with the United States Coast Guard in 1939.

Today, more efficient types of navigational aids have left most lighthouses playing a secondary role in navigation. While the Coast Guard is still responsible for many active lighthouses, these are becoming fewer in number as advancements in technology render them obsolete. As a result, more local governments and other non-profit groups are working with the Coast Guard in taking responsibility for maintenance of lighthouses and using them as educational or recreational facilities.

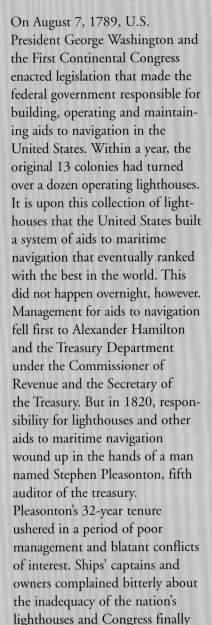

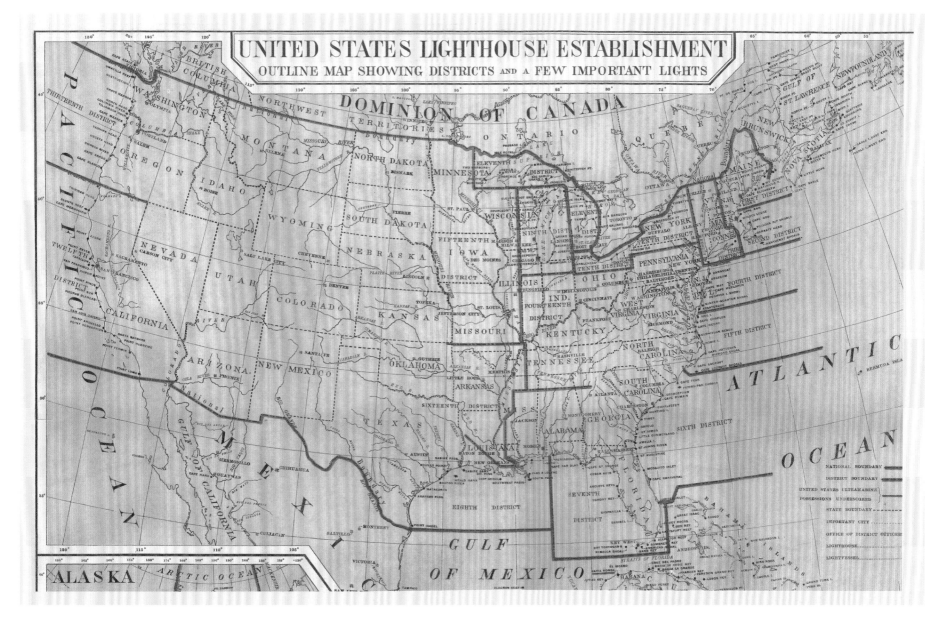

United States Lighthouse Establishment District Map of the lower 48 States, ca. 1914. At this time, the country was divided into 16 Lighthouse Districts in the United States. By the mid-1920s, districts were rearranged into 19 geographical regions that included Hawaii, Puerto Rico and adjacent islands.
Map from the D.J. Terras Collection

# Lighthouse Preservation

One section of the third-order Fresnel lens from Chicago's 1893 lighthouse. Today what remains of this historic lens lies crated and in storage at Point Cabrillo National Monument near San Diego, CA. Photo by D.J. Terras

The year 1989 marked the 200th anniversary of the founding of what came to be known as the United States Lighthouse Service. Although the Lighthouse Service was no longer in existence, many lighthouse enthusiasts from around the country flocked to Washington D.C. where a celebration was held to commemorate the occasion. One of the by-products of this event was the creation of a bicentennial U.S. Lighthouse Preservation Fund that sent thousands of dollars in federal money to aid preservation and restoration projects at historic American lighthouses. This special grant program lasted only three years but it gave a tremendous boost to the lighthouse preservation move-ment and set the stage for increased federal funding opportunities for lighthouses. More importantly, it served to usher in what became the most significant decade in history for lighthouse preservation.

For many years prior to the 1990s, historic lighthouses languished as improvements in technology rendered an increasing number of the old towers obsolete. Over time, they became a considerable maintenance headache for the U.S. Coast Guard that lacked the personnel necessary to properly care for these structures and the optics they contained. A few light-houses were transferred from federal to local jurisdiction, receiving better treatment at the hands of people who lived in the communities where the lighthouses were constructed. Generally, these lighthouses were simply maintained and did not attain the stature of symbols representing maritime history until recently. The formation of special interest groups like The Great Lakes Lighthouse Keepers Association in 1982, the U.S. Lighthouse Society in 1984 and the American Lighthouse Foundation in 1990, has helped tremendously. These organizations have been instrumental in generating public support for light-house preservation and education, and have acted to help get legislation passed that would benefit these historic structures.

Shedd Aquarium Lighthouse Exhibit. Photo by D.J. Terras

The 1990s also saw the John G. Shedd Aquarium in Chicago develop a special exhibition tracing the history and development of lighthouses. The Chicago aquarium is the largest indoor facility of its kind in the world and plays host to more than two million people on an annual basis. The exhibits and educational programs at the Shedd are internationally known and it's important that such an institution recognized the growing interest of lighthouses among the public with this popular exhibit. It was a further sign that lighthouses could be viewed outside of their strictly functional capacity and become educational tools, helping to tell the story of maritime navigation and exploration of the world's oceans, seas and inland waterways.

Lighthouse preservation was at a high point during this time as the general public became increasingly aware of the important role these sentinels have played in the development of maritime commerce and spread of cultures around the world. At the federal level, a National Maritime Initiative Program was created within the National Park Service to research and report on historic maritime resources of the United States. Their work continues today and has led to more lighthouses being added to the National Register of Historic Places and several others being designated as National Historic Landmarks.

In 1997, a steering committee was formed with the mission to find a suitable location for a National Lighthouse Museum. It was announced in July of 1998 that the museum would be located on New York's Staten Island in the city of St. George and would occupy the site and buildings of the old U.S. Lighthouse Depot established there in 1863. Shortly after, the State of Michigan, in association with the Great Lakes Lighthouse Keepers Association, announced plans to establish a Great Lakes Lighthouse Museum in Mackinac. The city of Rockland, Maine, has followed with the opening of The Maine Lighthouse Museum. The fact that these large lighthouse museums are being planned or have opened is further evidence of the momentum generated by the lighthouse movement toward education.

As a result of completing their mission, the National Lighthouse Museum Steering Committee was dissolved in 1998 and an American Lighthouse Coordinating Committee was formed from the composition of the group. This committee includes professionals from various fields of study representing different regions of the country whose topical area of interest has become lighthouses. The committee's general mission is to act

One of the finest collections of Fresnel lenses was put together by Ken Black, USCGR, and now resides in the Maine Lighthouse Museum in Rockland, ME.
Photo by D.J. Terras

as an advocacy group that is a natural extension of the interest in lighthouse preservation and education.

Today, public support and interest in using historic lighthouses for educational purposes continues to grow along with the preservation movement. As a result, many historic lighthouses left abandoned and lightless are once again shining with renewed public interest in their irreplaceable historic role as guardians of life at sea and symbols of maritime heritage around the world.

Membership in any of the organizations listed here will help continue lighthouse preservation and ensure their survival in the future.

American Lighthouse Foundation
P.O. Box 889
Wells, Maine 04090

Great Lakes Lighthouse Keepers
Association
P.O Box 219
206 Lake St.
Mackinaw City, MI 49701

National Lighthouse Center and
Museum
One Lighthouse Plaza
Staten Island, NY 10304

U.S. Lighthouse Society
244 Kearny St. - 5th Floor
San Francisco, CA 94108

# Historic Maritime Navigational Lights of Chicago

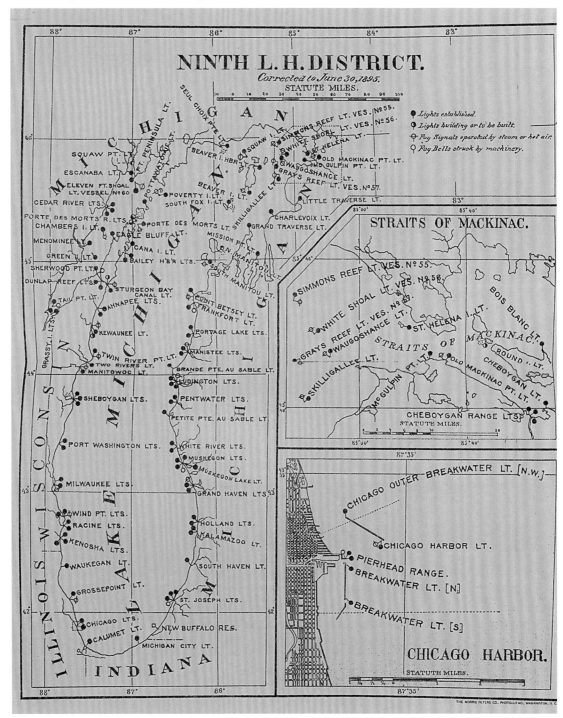

Ninth Lighthouse District Map. Annual
Report of Lighthouse Board, 1895.
From the National Archives

## Chicago Harbor Light
Location: Near southeast end of outer breakwater
Beacon: Flashing red and white,
Red flash: 0.7 sec.; Eclipse 9.3 sec.; White flash 0.7 sec.; Eclipse 9.3 sec.
Visibility: 16 miles
Candlepower: 22,000 Red; 31,000 White
Structure: Red, conical tower
12-inch steam whistle:
3-second blast; 27 seconds of silence
Top of lantern is 66 feet above base

## Municipal Pier #2 Light
Location: On southeast corner of pier
Beacon: Occulting red, 4 seconds
Light: 2 sec.; Eclipse: 2 sec.
Visibility: 10 miles
Candlepower: 160
Structure: Green; round skeleton mast
Top of lantern is 28 feet above base
Maintained by City of Chicago

## Chicago Pierhead Front Range Light
Location: On outer end of pier
Beacon: Fixed Red
Visibility: 8 miles
Candlepower: 50
Structure: White oval tower
Top of lantern is 28 feet above base

## Chicago Pierhead Rear Range Light
Location: 36 yards 271 degrees 10 feet from front range light
Beacon: Fixed White
Visibility: 12 miles
Candlepower: 350
Structure: White cylindrical tower
Top of lantern is 41 feet above base
Fog/Warning Bell:
2 strokes, 20 seconds; 1 stroke, 20 seconds

## Chicago Breakwater North Light
Location: Northeast angle of inner breakwater
Beacon: Flashing White, 3 seconds
Flash: 1-second duration
Visibility: 8 miles
Candlepower: 70
Structure: White pyramidal skeleton tower
Top of lantern is 22 feet above base

## Chicago Breakwater South Light
Location: South end of north section of inner breakwater
Beacon: Occulting Red, 2 seconds
Flash: Light 1 second; Eclipse 1 second
Visibility: 10 miles
Candlepower: 100
Structure: Gray, conical tower
Top of lantern is 33 feet above base

## Four-Mile Crib Light
Location: 3 3/4 miles off Grant Park
Beacon: Fixed White
Visibility: 10 miles
Candlepower: 160
Structure: Lantern on crib
Top of lantern is 42 feet above base
Fog/Warning Bell:
1 stroke every 10 seconds
Maintained by City of Chicago

## Hyde Park Crib Light
Location: 2 miles off Jackson Park, Chicago
Beacon: Fixed White
Visibility: 10 miles
Candlepower: 160
Structure: Lantern on crib
Top of lantern is 50 feet above base
Fog/Warning Bell:
1 stroke every 12 seconds
Maintained by City of Chicago

## Edward F. Dunne Crib Light
Location: 40 yards south of Hyde Park Crib
Beacon: Fixed Red
Visibility: 4 miles
Candlepower: 10
Structure: Lantern on crib
Maintained by City of Chicago

## Chicago Waterworks (Two-Mile) Crib Light
Location: On crib
Beacon: Fixed White
Visibility: 10 miles
Candlepower: 120
Structure: Lantern on crib
Top of lantern is 56 feet above base
Fog/Warning Bell:
1 stroke every 12 seconds
Maintained by City of Chicago

## Carter H. Harrison Crib Light
Location: On crib
Beacon: Fixed White
Visibility: 12 miles
Candlepower: 280
Structure: Tower attached to waterworks building
Top of lantern is 31 feet above base
Fog/Warning Bell:
1 stroke every 20 seconds
Maintained by City of Chicago

## Lakeview Crib Light
Location: On crib
Beacon: Fixed White
Visibility: 10 miles
Candlepower: 160
Structure: Lantern on waterworks crib
Top of lantern is 17 feet above base
Fog/Warning Bell: Every 30 seconds
Maintained by City of Chicago

## Wilson Avenue Intake Crib Light
Location: 1,970 yards from Lakeview Crib
Beacon: Fixed White
Visibility: Not Available
Candlepower: 60
Structure: Post on platform
Fog/Warning Bell:
1 stroke every 15 seconds
Maintained by City of Chicago

## Lawrence Avenue Crib Light
Location: On crib
Beacon: Fixed Red
Visibility: 8 miles
Candlepower: 50
Structure: Post on crib
Maintained by City of Chicago

## Calumet Harbor Light
Location: On southeast end of breakwater
Beacon: Fixed White with alternating Red
Flash of 0.6 sec. duration every 15 seconds
Visibility: 13 miles
Candlepower: White, 1,700; Red, 6,700
Structure: Light tower; Buff; cylindrical, attached to fog signal building
Top of lantern is 39 feet above base
1st class air siren:
2 blasts every 60-seconds; 3 sec. blast; 12 sec. silence; 3 sec. blast;42 sec. silence.

## Calumet Pierhead Light
Location: On outer end of north pier
Beacon: Fixed Red
Visibility: 9 miles
Candlepower: 80
Structure: Gray, cylindrical light tower
Top of lantern is 35 feet above base
Fog/Warning Bell:
1-stroke every 20-seconds

# Chicago Harbor and Lighthouse Timeline     1673

**1673** Jacques Marquette and Louis Joliet chart the area that is to become Chicago. Joliet makes a note about its strategic location in his diary.

**1803** Fort Dearborn is constructed on the banks of the Chicago River to create a military presence in the area and help promote trade.

**1812** Massacre at Fort Dearborn and destruction of the fort by Native Americans.

**1816** Fort Dearborn is reconstructed on the south shore of the Chicago River.

**1831-32** Chicago's first lighthouse was made from rubblestone and built near Fort Dearborn overlooking the Chicago River and Lake Michigan.

**1835** A channel was dredged through sandbars blocking the entrance to Chicago Harbor and two piers were constructed 200 feet apart for access to the river.

**1837** Chicago was incorporated as a city on March 4.

**1847** The north pier at Chicago's harbor was extended to 3,900 feet and a pole beacon light erected for navigation.

**1848** Completion of the Illinois-Michigan Canal took 12 years and created an inland water-borne transportation system from the Great Lakes to the Illinois and Mississippi Rivers south to the Gulf of Mexico.

**1849** $15,000 was appropriated for a light station on the end of the north pier that was later referred to as the Chicago River Light.

**1851** First lighthouse to mark South Chicago's Calumet River Harbor was commissioned by the federal government.

**1852** Pile-designed light constructed about 50 feet north of the end of the north pier at Chicago River entrance.

Creation of a Lighthouse Board by the federal government to oversee the construction and administration of lighthouses along the shores of the United States.

**1853** Completion and activation of South Chicago's Calumet Harbor Lighthouse.

**1855** Calumet's light was deactivated because of difficulties distinguishing it from Chicago's light.

**1859** Activation of screwpile lighthouse tower at entrance to Chicago River Harbor, first approved in 1849. Also, the 1831-32 masonry light tower was deactivated.

**1863** Calumet Harbor joins the Chicago Harbor system, comprised of Chicago River Harbor, Calumet River Harbor, and a new harbor development at Lake Calumet.

**1866-67** Construction of Chicago's first water works crib with lighthouse was completed November 30, 1866 and began operation March 25, 1867 two miles from Lake Michigan's shoreline.

**1869** North Pier was extended requiring additional lights to mark the Chicago Harbor port entrance.

**1871** $10,000 is appropriated for re-establishing a lighthouse at Calumet.

The flow of the Chicago River is reversed through a connection with the Illinois and Michigan Canal. Lake Michigan water helps to purify what had become a greatly polluted river.

Great Chicago Fire, October 8-9

**1873** The Calumet Lighthouse is reactivated and a light at the outer end of Calumet River's north pier completed on Feb. 10.

Chicago's leading light is re-located at Grosse Point in Evanston, IL, some 12 miles north of the harbor entrance..

**1874** Grosse Point Light begins operation on March 1 as the leading navigational aid into the Port of Chicago.

**1876** The addition of a breakwater at Chicago's river harbor created the need for two additional beacons to mark the ends of the structure.

Calumet's shoreline light was deactivated and moved to the end of the river's north pier.

**1888** The need for additional fresh water forced Chicago to construct a water works crib–complete with light tower–four miles offshore. Several other water intake cribs would be constructed in following years.

**1890** The addition of another (south) breakwater at Chicago River Harbor required the installation of beacon-type pole lights at the ends of the structure to aid navigation.

**1893** World's Columbian Exposition at Chicago included the construction and operation of a lighthouse staffed by five keepers that was displayed throughout the course of the event.

Construction of a new light station at the end of a breakwater close to the north pier. This light was officially designated as Chicago Harbor Light and contained a third-order Fresnel lens.

**1893** The 1859 Chicago Harbor Lighthouse was dismantled and the primary watchroom and lantern used in the construction of Twin River (Rawley Point) lighthouse WI..

**1893** Carter Harrison Water Intake Crib Lighthouse is completed.

**1898** Calumet's wooden lighthouse on the north pier was demolished and replaced with a new light tower made from cast iron.

**1900** The opening of the Chicago Sanitary and Ship Canal completely reversed the flow of the Chicago river from Lake Michigan inland. This feat has been recognized by many historians to be one of the technological wonders of the Industrial Age.

**1903** Chicago breakwater south light tower constructed.

**1906** Chicago pierhead range lights are constructed on north pier.

**1906** Calumet Harbor (South Chicago) Lighthouse was constructed on a 7,000-foot breakwater and worked with the pierhead light to aid ships navigating into port.

**1907** Chicago's north breakwater light tower was completed and put in operation.

**1910** United States Lighthouse Board is replaced by the United States Bureau of Lighthouses.

**1915** The passenger liner Eastland overturns at dockside in the Chicago River with the death of 815 people.

**1918** To enhance the effectiveness of Chicago Harbor Light, the station is moved to a crib foundation at the end of a breakwater, 1/2 mile from the end of Navy Pier.

**1923** In an effort to technologically upgrade all lighthouses in the Ninth Lighthouse District, Chicago Harbor Lighthouse and those at Calumet are electrified.

**1938** Navigation into the Chicago River is enhanced with construction of Chicago Harbor Southeast Guidewall Light.

**1939** U.S. Bureau of Lighthouses/Lighthouse Service is merged with the U.S. Coast Guard.

**1959** Opening of the St. Lawrence Seaway connecting the Great Lakes directly to the Atlantic Ocean. Chicago becomes an international port.

**1963** Original third-order Fresnel lens is removed from Chicago Harbor Light and moved to Point Loma, CA, near San Diego.

**1976** Calumet's historic 1898 pierhead light is struck by a ship and demolished.

**1995** Calumet's 1906 breakwater light is demolished by the Coast Guard.

**2005** Chicago Harbor Lighthouse remains an active aid to maritime navigation, but the buildings have become excess property. The U.S. Government opens discussions with organizations and individuals suitable to act as stewards of this landmark structure.

# Major Bibliographical References

In addition to references cited within the text, the following list of publications provided important information in documenting the story of Chicago's lighthouses, tall ships, and its era as the most important port on the Great Lakes.

*A History of Chicago*
Department of Public Works, City of Chicago
Rand McNally & Co., 1973

Andreas, Alfred T.
*History of Chicago*
1884-86 3-vols. Chicago

Annual Reports of the Lighthouse Board (Cited in text)
Washington, DC,
Government Printing Office

Annual Report of the U.S. Life-Saving Service, 1894
Washington, DC,
Government Printing Office

Barry, James P.
*Ships of the Great Lakes*
1973, Thunder Bay Press

Bass, George F.
*Ships and Shipwrecks of the Americas*
Thames and Hudson, 1988

Blanchard, Rufus
*Discovery and Conquests of the Northwest*
R. Blanchard and Co.
1881

Buisseret, David
*Historic Illinois From the Air*
University of Chicago Press, 1990

Burgess, Arnold
*Exhibit of the Light-House Board*
In Appendix to Annual Report of the Lighthouse Board, 1894

Cameron, William
*The World's Fair*
Chicago Publications and Lithograph Co. 1893

Chamberlain, Everett,
*Chicago and Its Suburbs*
T.A. Hungerford & Co. 1874

Clifford, Candace
*Inventory of Historic Light Stations*
National Park Service, 1994

City of Chicago
*Report of Public Works to the City Council*, Chicago, IL 1862, 1863, 1864, 1865, 1866, 1868, 1870, 1876, 1880, 1888, 1889, 1890, 1891, 1892

Dornfeld, A.A.
"Chicago's Age of Sail"
*Chicago History*, Spring/Summer 1973, Chicago Historical Society

Dornfeld, A.A.
"Steamships after 1871"
*Chicago History*, Spring 1977
Chicago Historical Society

Gordon, Anne
"Investigating the Eastland Disaster"
*Chicago History*, 1981
Chicago Historical Society

Grossman, J. & Karamanski, T. Ed
*Historic Lighthouses and Navigational Aids of the Illinois Shore of Lake Michigan*
Illinois Historic Preservation Agency, 1989

Hatcher, H. & E. Walter
*Pictorial History of the Great Lakes*
Bonanza Books, NY, 1953

Hyde, Charles C.
*The Northern Lights*
Two Peninsula Press
1996

Lafferty, William
"Yesterday's City: Excursion on the Lakefront"
*Chicago History*
Fall and Winter, 1991-92,
Chicago Historical Society

Light, Judith L.
"Automation Creeps Up On Men
Who Tend Lake Lights"
*Chicago Daily News*
January 5, 1963

Mansfield, J.B.
*History of the Great Lakes*
J.H. Beers and Co., 1899

Miller, Donald L.
*City of the Century: The Epic of
Chicago and the Making of America*
Simon & Schuster, New York, 1996

National Archives, Record Group 26,
U.S. Lighthouse Establishment
a) General Correspondence Files
b) Field Records
c) Descriptive lists of light stations
   (Site Files)
    1. Descriptive lists of lighthouses
       in 11th District, 1858
    2. Description of Calumet
       Pierhead Light Station, 1909
    3. Description of Calumet Harbor
       Breakwater Light Station, 1909
    4. Description of Chicago Harbor
       Light Station, 1929
d) Lighthouse Logs (Chicago Harbor)
e) Journals of the Lighthouse Board
f) Correspondence, 1853 to 1923

No Author Listed
"Nation to Observe 150th Birthday of
Lighthouse Service"
*Chicago Daily News*
July 26, 1939

No Author Listed
"Our Coast Beacons"
*The Chicago Inter-Ocean*
Sunday, November 9, 1890 V.19, No.
229

Noble, Dennis
Lighthouses and Keepers
Naval Institute Press, 1997

O'Brien, Michael T. and Dennis L.
Noble
"Heroes on Ninety Cents a Day"
*Inland Seas*
Great Lakes Historical Society Volume
33 (1977)

Recktenwald, William
"The Guiding Light"
*Chicago Tribune*
Sunday, December 13, 1992

*Sailing Directions for the Great Lakes
and Connecting Waters*
Hydrographic Office, Navy
Department, 1896

Terras, Donald,
*Grosse Point Lighthouse: Landmark to
Maritime History and Culture*
Windy City Press, 1995

————————————

National Historic Landmark
Nomination:
*Grosse Point Lighthouse*
Department of the Interior, National
Park Service, Maritime Initiatives
Program 1998

Thiersch, Hermann
*Pharos Antik Islam und Occident*
1909, Leipzig und Berlin

Weiss, George
*The Lighthouse Service*
Johns Hopkins Press, 1926

*The Great Lakes: An Environmental
Atlas and Resource Book*
Government of Canada and United
States Environmental Protection
Agency, 1995

# About the Author

Photo by Beckermedia.com

**Donald J. Terras**

Donald J. Terras has worked in the field of historic and cultural resource management for over 20 years in a broad range of public and private institutions. During this time, he's received awards from several organizations that include the American Association for State and Local History and Landmarks Preservation Council of Illinois. In addition, he's a recipient of the Professional of the Year Award from the Illinois Association of Museums.

Mr. Terras is director of the Lighthouse Park District in Evanston, IL, and the District-operated Grosse Point Lighthouse National Landmark. He is a member of the National Historic Landmark Steward's Committee and serves on the board of the American Lighthouse Coordinating Committee, a national lighthouse preservation and education leadership council. A graduate of the University of Wisconsin program in Museum Studies, Mr. Terras also holds a Master of Science degree in anthropology. He has taught museum studies at both the University of Wisconsin and Northeastern Illinois University.